Linni
524 D
S0-EOH-160

COMPASS HISTORY OF ART

Medieval Manuscript Painting

Compass History of Art

Edited by André Held and D. W. Bloemena

The complete series comprises:

Greek Painting

Roman and Ètruscan Painting

Early Christian Painting

Byzantine and Early Medieval Painting

Romanesque Painting

Gothic Painting

Medieval Manuscript Painting

Renaissance Painting

Seventeenth-Century Painting

Eighteenth-Century Painting

Nineteenth-Century Painting

Twentieth-Century Painting

Medieval Manuscript Painting

Sabrina Mitchell

THE VIKING PRESS
New York

© 1964 by J. M. Meulenhoff, Amsterdam
Text © 1965 by George Weidenfeld and Nicolson Ltd
Photographs © 1964 by André Held

A COMPASS BOOKS original edition
Published in 1965 by The Viking Press, Inc.
625 Madison Avenue, New York, N.Y. 10022
Library of Congress catalog card number: 64–21645
Printed in Holland

Contents

Introduction 1

Romanesque Manuscript Illumination 3

Background – Ottonian Painting – Germany – England – Spain – Italy – France

Gothic Manuscript Illumination 21

The Transition from Romanesque to Gothic – France – England – Germany – Bohemia – Italy

The International Gothic Style 33

France – England – Italy – Bohemia

René d'Anjou 41

Fifteenth-Century Flemish Illumination 42

Jean Fouquet and Later French Illumination 43

Illustrations

Captions

Introduction

Manuscript illumination of the Middle Ages is of special importance in the study of the pictorial art of the period. Great numbers of wall-paintings have perished, faded or been destroyed by sunlight, damp and vandalism; the technique of oil-painting was not discovered until the fifteenth century, and there are only fragmentary remains of the great stained-glass windows that adorned so many cathedrals and abbeys. In contrast, the small size of manuscripts enabled them to be stored in the comparative safety of libraries, each illustration shut away from the light and the volumes bound between strong covers. These illustrations, which bear witness to the flowering of medieval art, can be seen in a very good state of preservation even today. Moreover, the illumination of manuscripts is by no means a minor art. The paintings are not a mere reflection of larger wall paintings; indeed, it is known that manuscripts were often copied by fresco painters and their influence can be seen in the work of some medieval sculptors. They are, despite their size, often monumental works of art.

Before the invention of printing, books were the precious possessions of great ecclesiastical or secular patrons, produced only after long hours, even months, of fine, patient work. During the earlier part of the period the books were written and illustrated in monastic foundations by monks working in the part of the abbey called the scriptorium. The manuscripts were written solely 'for the Greater Glory of God', and commissions from kings and emperors were considered acts of piety and religious devotion. Later, however, the patronage changed and during the thirteenth century we see knights and noblemen commissioning books for their own private use. Guilds of illuminators were founded and the writing and illustrating of manuscripts became a commercial enterprise with properly organized workshops, commissions and payments.

The pages offer the widest possible range of subject-matter and from them we can glean information about the manners and customs of medieval people. Every aspect of their lives is illustrated. Different types of armour and methods of making war are there for the student to examine as well as the musical instruments they used, the games they played and the clothes they wore. Many different types of books were illuminated. First, there are the ceremonial books for use during church services. Apart from the Bible there are Gospel Books and Evangeliaries which contain the Canon Tables at the beginning showing a concordance of texts from the four Gospels; there are Missals, Breviaries, Benedictionals and Psalters for conducting the services and special books such as the Gradual which contains passages to be sung on the altar steps. Then there are the treatises intended for theological instruction such as the commentaries of Abbot Liebana on the Apocalypse, St Jerome's commentary on the Psalms or St Augustine's *De Civitate Dei.* Monks proudly commemorated saints from their monasteries by writing accounts of their lives. Certain non-religious works like the comedies of Terence and the Caedmon poems appeared during the Romanesque period along with encyclopedic works on medicine, animals and plants, but it is during the fourteenth and fifteenth centuries that secular books became really fashionable. With changes of patronage, we move into the Age of Chivalry, the age of the great romances of Lancelot du Lac, the *Roman de la Rose* and the poems of Christine de Pisan.

These manuscripts come down to us today as representatives of a lost way of life and thought. Nothing had greater significance for that age than religion. The laborious creation of a manuscript was an exercise in faith, thought to be beneficial to the illuminator. For the reader, it was equally rewarding, spiritually.

The very survival in perfect state of any object of this age is of interest in itself. Manuscripts are examples of work done solely by hand. No artist's paper or sketchbooks were handed to these craftsmen. The task began with the preparation of fine vellum, very thin and yet strong. Colours of great purity and lasting intensity had to be obtained, ground and mixed; endless exact lines of script had to be faultlessly copied; gold leaf was delicately gilded and patterned on backgrounds. All this had to be done on a minute scale requiring perfect concentration and control. The often-quoted saying 'Art is its own reward' could not be more justly applied to any other branch of art. Illuminated manuscripts are the superb combination of artistry, craftsmanship and religious devotion.

The scope of this book covers the period from *c* 1000 to *c* 1500 and includes the whole of Western Europe. It is a period stretching from before the Norman Conquest to the reign of Henry VII in England, from the Ottonian Empire in Germany to the High Renaissance in Italy. Crusades were undertaken against the Infidel, momentous battles lost and won, and during this time new horizons were opened up by the journeyings of Marco Polo, Columbus and Vasco da Gama. The history of manuscript illumination between 1000 and 1500 can be broken up into two very general groups, the Romanesque style and the Gothic style, but there is no precise dividing line between the two and, at the same time, each general title embraces a great number of different trends varying not only from country to country but also from one period of time to another. The Romanesque style spans the period from the Millennium until about 1200 when new trends consolidate to form the Gothic style.

In the simplest terms, Romanesque art must not be judged by the artist's ability to paint what he saw. The maxim of truth to nature does not apply as this was not the artist's intention. It is a highly sophisticated style that sacrifices optical veracity to narrative clarity. The Romanesque style is the creation of a people imbued with deep religious conviction, and if the artist felt that he could achieve wider emotional significance by stylizing the portrayal of the human figure, by taking him out of his earthly environment, he did not hesitate to do so. To obtain narrative impact the figures are sometimes drawn directly onto the bare parchment or set against a solid, brightly coloured background of gold or blue. The figures themselves are flattened into two dimensions and often clothed in draperies broken up into a pattern of geometric shapes.

However, when the centres of illumination moved from the seclusion of the cloister to the workshops and guilds, the style was already changing into the so-called Gothic manner. The new patronage demanded a different, more realistic style of painting to record its transitory, earthly riches for posterity. By the fifteenth century the art had reached the summit of a delicate, miniature representation of the world in which the artist lived. Landscape was treated with minute care and such a book as the *Très Riches Heures du Duc de Berry* is a milestone in the history of landscape-painting. The invention of the printing press was the death knell for the art of manuscript illumination, and in the West it stopped abruptly at the beginning of the sixteenth century.

Romanesque Manuscript Illumination

Background

Before the emergence of the Romanesque style, manuscript illumination had flourished under the auspices of the Emperor Charlemagne (768–814) and it was to Carolingian books that later artists turned for their inspiration. Earlier, some very fine books had been written and illustrated in Ireland and England at the beginning of the eighth century which show initials with an abundance of geometric interlace and designs worked with exquisite and minute care. Representations of the human figure, seen, for example, in the Lindisfarne Gospels in the British Museum, are complete stylizations with no feeling for depth or perspective. Irish monks travelled to Europe, taking their books with them, and this anti-figural style was still dominant in the many monasteries they founded right up to the time of Charlemagne.

Charlemagne, in his attempt to model himself on the Caesars and rival the Byzantine Emperors, showed a conscious desire to revive the Antique and gathered round him numerous advisors, scholars and artists. He welcomed the Greek painters who could no longer work for the Byzantine Emperors, and the theologian Alcuin of York was one of his trusted counsellors. Carolingian painting presents a synthesis of the different styles available to the artists and shows a combination of Byzantine influences, the Early Christian and Late Antique models of Italy, and the works carried abroad by the Irish missionaries and deposited in libraries at such places as St Gall in Switzerland, Bobbio in Italy, Fulda and Würzburg in Germany and Luxeuil and Tours in France.

It must be remembered that the Carolingian style was not bounded by the present-day frontier of any one country; it was a European style extending over a great area from Italy to the English Channel and beyond. Each scriptorium had its own special style, emphasizing one or another particular prototype. For instance, the scriptorium at Reims produced books illustrated with scratchy line drawings that owe much to Early Christian examples, whereas the so-called Palace School at Aachen produced lavish psalters written on rich purple vellum in direct imitation of books of the Byzantine Emperors. We must not forget that the presence of a single manuscript in a monastery could have a very strong influence on the work of a whole generation, a fact that will become self-evident in the discussion of English eleventh-century manuscripts of the south of England. For all its diversity, Carolingian art has an international character that will not be seen again until the appearance of the so-called International Gothic style of the fifteenth century.

Ottonian Painting

The Carolingian Empire went into decline late in the ninth century, and eventually Western Europe was divided into a number of distinct countries; the late tenth century and the early eleventh century see the emergence of individual, national styles. The mantle of Charlemagne fell onto the shoulders of the Ottonian dynasty in Germany in 936. These Ottonian Emperors modelled themselves closely on their great predecessor and the Ottonian Renaissance is in many respects a revival of Carolingian ideals. The Emperors were great patrons of the arts and were fortunate to have intelligent bishops like Egbert of Trier and Bernward of

Hildesheim to encourage their artistic interests. It was the Emperors themselves who commissioned great books to be written, and although the manuscripts were not destined for the patron himself, certain scriptoria became noted for their fine work and books written there were presented to other abbeys as an act of devotion on the part of the Emperor. This enlightened patronage gave rise to a very fine school of manuscript illumination.

Despite the fascination of the Carolingian achievements, Ottonian painting is not simply a lifeless copying of its works. Many novel features emerge and there is a new emphasis on the use of line; there is a new interrelation of figure, background and border, and the picture surface is intentionally flattened to give a stronger narrative impact. However, the interest in ancient prototypes and Byzantine art is reaffirmed, purple vellum or painted purple backgrounds are used and books are often bound in Byzantine ivory covers.

A Sacramentary from Fulda in the University Library at Tübingen (fig. 1), written and illustrated in the tenth century, shows an interesting transition from the Carolingian to the later Ottonian style. It has a calendar page showing figures that represent the Four Seasons surrounding a central medallion which contains a symbol of the Year. The borders contain the Labours of the Months. The figures are swathed in toga-like draperies that suggest a knowledge of Late Classical painting, so popular in Carolingian times, but the total lack of any background perspective hints at the impending changes in Romanesque art.

Several main centres of illumination flourished in Germany under the Ottonian dynasty (936–1024). Perhaps the most important school was situated at Reichenau on Lake Constance, but others flourished at Trier and Echternach in the valley of the Moselle, at Regensburg on the Danube and at Cologne on the Rhine. The style of painting that developed at these places during the late tenth century and early eleventh century was to last long after the end of the Ottonian Empire, and it formed the basis of German manuscript illumination until the advent of the new Gothic style towards the end of the twelfth century.

In the tenth century the monastery at Reichenau probably had books of the Late Classical period in its possession. The Codex Egberti (Trier, Stadtbibliothek), a Gospel book written for Archbishop Egbert of Trier *c* 980, contains a series of illustrations in the text that reflect the quiet repose of Early Christian and Late Classical works. It has pale pastel colours and a certain purity of line. The hands of more than one artist were employed, but it seems that the most classical artist was the inspiration for the others. Stylistic evidence suggests that this master soon moved to Trier, possibly at the personal request of Egbert, as this manner of painting does not persist at Reichenau.

A much more characteristic book is another work commissioned by Archbishop Egbert, the Psalter now in the museum at Cividale del Friuli, Italy. This Psalter, known as the Egbert Psalter or the Codex Gertrudianus, has thirty-seven full-page illustrations showing portraits of fourteen of Egbert's predecessors, paintings of the donors and large illuminated initials. The figure of the monk (fig. 2), probably Ruodpreht the illuminator, is set against a solid background of red instead of the shaded grounds of the Codex Egberti, and the folds of the drapery do nothing to increase the reality of a kneeling man. The picture of St Uitvino (fig. 4) shows the bishop standing in the position of a Byzantine Orant and the area behind him is filled with a grille studded with foliage motifs; both the donor and the bishop are enclosed in a formal border of dazzling gold. The coloured backgrounds seem to be imitations of the precious purple vellum of the books of the Byzantine Emperors. The initials of this work are equally lavish and letter 'B' of the word 'Beatus' (fig. 3) fills a whole page. Again it is placed on a patterned ground and at each projection the foliage of the infillings spreads out in a tight interlace to grasp the border; the colours glow with the brilliance of enamels.

The Gospels in Florence (Biblioteca Laurenziana) are laid out in characteristic format. The first six openings of the book are filled with the Eusebian Canons, relating the corresponding passages from the four Gospels. At the beginning of each of the Gospels is a full-page illustration of the Evangelist seated at his desk with the symbolic representation behind; St John the Evangelist (fig. 7) is seen in just such a manner. In addition to these standard illustrations this book has a painting of the Ascension (fig. 6). Both paintings reveal a compromise between the Codex Egberti and the Psalter in Cividale del Friuli. The figures are set against a shaded ground to suggest pictorial perspective and yet the rounded hillocks in the Ascension are formalized to produce an entirely decorative effect. The faces have a latent visionary, introspective quality that is more fully conveyed in two slightly later books: the Gospel Book and the Apocalypse written for Emperor Henry II and his wife as a gift for the cathedral at Bamberg between 1002 and 1014.

The scenes from the Life of Christ in the Gospel Book (fig. 9) show another step away from the classical tradition, for here the background is now divided into three bands of solid colour, so that there is no longer any conception of depth; the figures and draperies are drawn with a hard, flat precision. Scenes from the Apocalypse are admirably suited to this visionary manner of painting, which sacrifices much to obtain dramatic impact. The Vision of the New Jerusalem (fig. 12) in the Bamberg Apocalypse is reduced to its bare essentials, thus ensuring a most striking effect. The figures are set against a solid ground of gold, and the scene is drawn with a remarkable economy of line.

Perhaps the most serene subjects in Ottonian manuscripts can be found in a group of works written under the auspices of Archbishop Egbert at Trier. The sobriety of the *Codex Egberti* from Reichenau has already been noted and it seems that one of its masters went with Egbert to Trier. Books in this group can be found today in the Bibliothèque Nationale and the Sainte Chapelle Library in Paris, also in Aachen and in Prague, but it is headed by the works of the so-called Master of the Registrum Gregorii. Only two pages survive from this manuscript. The first of these shows St Gregory in his study watched by the deacon Petrus (Trier, Stadtbibliothek) (fig. 5). St Gregory is set in a small building and is separated from his servant by a draped curtain supported on classical pillars. The simple outlines and solid structure of the scene give this painting an entirely different feeling from the flat but expressive forms of the Psalter written at Reichenau for the same archbishop. The other fragment of this book, which is now kept at Chantilly (Musée Condé), shows an enthroned Emperor, either Otto III or Otto II, holding an orb and sceptre (fig. 8). The Emperor is surrounded by four allegorical figures of women who represent the subject countries of the Ottonian Empire. This is modelled on the books of the Byzantine rulers and we must not forget that the homage paid to Byzantium led to marriages with Byzantine princesses and to the employment of their scholars as tutors in the royal household.

Echternach is situated only a short distance up the river Moselle from Trier, and the interaction of influences is hardly unexpected. A comparison between the Lectionary in Brussels (Bibliothèque Royale) (fig. 10) and the Chantilly page from the Registrum Gregorii (fig. 8) shows some similarities. Both scriptoria used architectural settings and simple drapery, but the treatment of the Echternach manuscript is harsher, the colours more bold and there is a far more superficial understanding of the classical prototypes. Here, for instance, the capitals on the little building are decorated with strange grotesques, rather than Corinthian acanthus. It is not known where the Evangeliary at Brescia (Biblioteca Queriniana) came from, but evidence points to Echternach. The illustrations of this book (figs. 14 and 15) seem to be of a slightly later date than the Brussels Lectionary, with influence from Reichenau present in the gold grounds and the harsher draperies. Despite the high quality of the books from Echternach, the style lacks the dazzling invention of the Reichenau school just as it lacks the purity of the Trier works.

The ideas that came to fruition at Reichenau had the greatest single impact on the other scriptoria in Germany. The indigenous style of Cologne, for example, was based on books from the Palace School of Charlemagne. The handling of the illustrations in a work such as the Hitda Codex of the Cologne School is loose and painterly. There are indications of beautiful landscapes and a naturalistic sense of colour. Then suddenly the style changed; the simplest explanation is the establishment of closer contacts with Reichenau. The Evangeliary of Abdinghof (Berlin, Kupferstichscabinett), for example, dates from the middle of the eleventh century. The painting of Christ giving his mission to the Apostles (figs. 16 and 17) shows figures drawn with bold lines and the stiff, powerful draperies of the earlier Reichenau style.

The scriptorium at Regensburg flourished in the monastery of St Emmeran under the patronage of the Emperor Henry II. The Carolingian books already there, notably the Codex Aureus of Charles the Bald, played a major role in the formation of the Regensburg style. The Sacramentary of Henry II (1002–1014) now in Munich (Staatsbibliothek) seems to be a direct interpretation of the Codex Aureus by an artist trained in Byzantium. St Gregory (fig. 20) has a purely Greek face with a sharp aquiline nose and the folds of his robe are drawn with crisp angular lines, yet the artist uses white to denote highlights, a heritage from Carolingian painting, and the foliage ornamenting the border gives a richly decorative effect. The Evangeliary of Abbess Uota of Niedermuster (Munich, Staatsbibliothek) which includes a page showing the Abbess offering her book to the Blessed Virgin Mary, must have been written between 1002 and 1035. The scenes have the same wealth of decorative ornamentation as the Sacramentary, but the Crucifixion (fig. 21) has a new symbolic character. The competence with which the paint is handled is of the highest order, but in place of the stark drama of the event, as seen in Reichenau books, we now have a symbolic figure of Christ surrounded by allegories of Light and Darkness, of Life and Death, and the figures of the soldiers at the foot of the Cross are supplanted by symbols of the Church and Synagogue.

Germany

When Henry III died in 1056, Germany entered on a long period of turmoil and conflict with the papacy. In this unsettled atmosphere the emperors had little time to commission books and the mainstream of royal patronage was interrupted. Scriptoria at such places as Reichenau and Regensburg faded away; at least the books produced there show a decline in quality, and new centres became important. During the Ottonian period the stylistic advances made in Germany tended to spread towards the West but after the middle of the eleventh century the position was to some extent reversed. The Ottonian style was modified by Western ideas. The Cluniac reforms brought new ideas to the monasteries in Swabia and Hirsau. Weingarten maintained a fine tradition of illumination during the whole of the twelfth century; its books show Anglo-Saxon and Flemish influence, probably because the Countess Judith of

Flanders presented the abbey, the family monastery of the Guelphs, with books from Flanders and from Southern England.

During the twelfth century Austria came to the forefront of developments in that part of Europe. Salzburg produced a large corpus of illuminated manuscripts and the best examples of its style can be seen in simple outline drawings executed in monochrome. New monasteries were founded and old monasteries were reformed in this area along the Danube; books from Admont and Mondsee, Zwettl, Heiligenkreuz and Klosterneuburg testify that this was a great age in Austrian miniature painting. The Zwiefalten Passional includes illuminations in which the artist can be seen struggling for powerful effects of plasticity although he still has recourse to earlier prototypes.

The abbey of Helmarshausen in Saxony was under the direct patronage of the uncrowned king of Northern Germany, Henry the Lion (1129–1195), and here again we see the growing increase of influence from the West, in particular from the Mosan area.

The spread of ideas did not confine itself to the western areas of Germany; for the manuscripts from Cluny must in part be responsible for the developments in Bohemia as early as 1085. Bohemia, which was to become a centre of great importance in later centuries, also produced a local school at this time. Among the examples of Bohemian painting are the Vysehrad Evangeliary (Prague, National University Library) and a copy of St Augustine's *De Civitate Dei* (Prague, Capitoline Library). The paintings in the Evangeliary (figs. 22 and 24) have the naïvety of popular art but the brushwork is handled with an assured rapidity that removes the illustrations to a higher plane. This is particularly noticeable in the St Augustine manuscript (fig. 23), which is more profound and shows a greater variety than the Evangeliary. From now on Bohemian painting became stylistically affiliated to the Rhineland.

Towards the end of the twelfth century the attempts at obtaining effects of plasticity and movement became far more satisfactory; this must in part be due to the second wave of Byzantine influence, full of humanity and naturalism, that revitalized the artistic developments in Germany, as elsewhere, and formed the basis of the Gothic style.

England

The style of manuscript illumination in England underwent a far more radical change during the eleventh and twelfth centuries than it did in Germany. In Germany, artists of the twelfth century turned again and again for their inspiration to Ottonian painting, but in English twelfth-century illumination only the native feeling for line survives from the Anglo-Saxon tradition.

As in Germany, the English artists of *c* 1000 were dependent on

Carolingian examples, but a compariso of two contemporary manuscripts from Winchester and Trier shows that each school chose a very different example to follow. The Registrum Gregorii at Trier (fig. 5) and the Benedictional of St Aethelwold (fig. 28) in the British Museum were illustrated at about the same date. In the Trier work a real attempt has been made to set the figures in space. Drapery is simple and contours are suggested by a few shaded lines; the illustration is rigidly confined within a sober border of solid colour. In contrast the scene of the Marys at the Sepulchre, from the Benedictional of St Aethelwold, seems complicated and untidy. Figures spread over into the borders and mingle with the acanthus foliage of the painted frame. Here emphasis is placed on line and the rapid, impressionistic drawing gives the illustration a sense of vitality and urgency very different from the sobriety of the German work.

Several different styles of Carolingian illumination were familiar to the artists of the early eleventh century, but it is significant that the Utrecht Psalter should have been the only work to make any great impact in England. This is a book abundantly illustrated with outline drawings and is known to have been at Canterbury during the Middle Ages. A direct copy of it was made *c* 1000 (London, British Museum) and in it one can see how perfectly this Carolingian style suited the indigenous feeling for calligraphic design.

Anglo-Saxon artists developed a style of their own that has seldom been surpassed in delicacy and vigour. This style is well illustrated in the books of Archbishop Robert of Jumièges (figs. 29–33). In all these, the acanthus foliage spreads unchecked in and around the frames of the illustration, earth and sky are suggested by rapid strokes of the brush, and everywhere the draperies look as if they are caught up by the wind. In a Psalter in the British Museum (fig. 34) the tragedy of the Crucifixion is beautifully expressed in this restless, delicate technique. Here there is no colour, merely the rapid strokes of a fine pen.

The conquest by the Normans in 1066 did not immediately affect the native style of manuscript illumination, but the Norman bishops brought foreign books with them and thus introduced new continental ideas. Gradually a harder, more painterly style emerged. A copy of St Augustine's *De Civitate Dei* (Florence, Biblioteca Laurenziana), illustrated at Canterbury in the early twelfth century, hints at the beginnings of a new style. In the small figures (figs. 26 and 27) the Anglo-Saxon drapery style remains and the figures seem as animated as ever, but the decoration of the border is more controlled, and the portrait of St Augustine is quite different. This is a figure set against a flat, patterned background; the hair is reduced to a formal coronet of curls, the stylized ear is shaped like a scallop shell and the drapery, particularly over the knees, is reduced to a solid block of geometric pattern.

The English manuscripts discussed so far originated from the scriptoria at Canterbury and Winchester, but now attention must be turned to St Albans and Bury St Edmunds. During the second quarter of the twelfth century a Psalter was illuminated at St Albans (now in the Hildesheim Godehard Dombibliothek) that was to have a decisive influence on the development of English Romanesque painting. The so-called Albani Psalter has over forty full-page illustrations as well as many decorated initials. In the paintings the figures are well spaced within the rigid framework of the surround and the elongated, monumental figures are now clothed in heavy hanging drapery that defines the body beneath it. The scenes are painted in strong, sombre colours, very different from the pale washed colours of Pre-Conquest manuscripts. Clearly the artists must have been strongly influenced by some Ottonian or Byzantine model. It is certain that this book was made at St Albans, but its influence at once extended to Bury St Edmunds, as can be seen in a Gospel book now at Pembroke College, Cambridge. The illuminations (fig. 38) are not strongly coloured as in the Albani Psalter, but the facial types and the new treatment of drapery owe much to the Albani Psalter. Several other English manuscripts betray the same influence, notably a Psalter written for the nuns of Shaftesbury (London, British Museum). On the whole, however, the Albani style proved too severe for English taste, and it was eventually superseded by more congenial alternatives.

In the middle of the twelfth century, a second copy was made at Canterbury from the Utrecht Psalter. The impressionistic realism has now been supplanted by pattern, the delicate flicks of the pen that suggested the ground have been replaced by formal shapes, the faces and drapery are reminiscent of the Albani style, and although the illustrations are still in outline, inks of several different colours have been used. Each scene is now confined within a patterned border, where before the figures were scattered around the text.

Among the finest books of the twelfth century is the great Bury Bible (Cambridge, Corpus Christi College). Bibles like this (fig. 37) offered new scope to artists, and were certainly famous even in their own day. The Bury Bible shows a total absorption of the Albani style. Figures are arranged in their setting with the same feeling for space, but here the drapery of the Albani Psalter has been developed in a characteristically English way, producing an effect of damp folds clinging to the form beneath. The paintings are executed in exquisitely bright colours and the pages gleam like jewels or enamels.

The 'damp fold' treatment of drapery, used almost realistically in the Bury Bible, was adapted by other painters into a more and more decorative abstraction. The Lambeth Bible, illustrated at Canterbury, shows the degree to which this schematization was taken, reducing the plastic form to flat geometric patterns. In the Bury Bible, the artist attempted to suggest depth by varying the background colours, as the Ottonian painters had done, but in the Lambeth Bible the figures are placed against a ground of solid colour. For those who think of Romanesque art as a conscious move away from realism, this must surely be a major work.

There is stylistic evidence to suggest that certain artists travelled from one scriptorium to another. At Winchester, another great Bible bears witness to this. Today it is bound in three volumes and presents a synthesis of the development of painting during the latter half of the twelfth century. It is probable that this book was illuminated at St Swithuns, Winchester, and parts of it compare closely with another Winchester book – the St Swithuns Psalter (London, British Museum) – but in the Bible the work of at least six different illuminators can be distinguished. The earliest of these, the so-called Master of the Leaping Figures, painted figures with a great sense of movement and vigour, using the 'damp fold' convention in a manner akin to that of the master of the Bury Bible. An almost contemporary artist, the Master of the Apocrypha Drawings (fig. 40), displays a crisper feeling for line and, it seems, intended his designs to be heightened with only a pale wash of colour. The later illustrations of the book are markedly different and show a decisive Byzantine influence. There were direct contacts between England and Sicily during the third quarter of the twelfth century, while the realism and classicism of the latest artist, appropriately known as The Master of the Gothic Majesty, heralds the birth of a new kind of figure art to which the name Gothic is applied. The first outstanding achievements of this new realism are to be found in the Westminster Psalter (London, British Museum), *c* 1200, in which five full-page paintings show figures designed with a new solidity and strength. The new style also appears in a Bestiary (London, British Museum) (fig. 39), in which all the formalized drapery conventions of the Romanesque style have been abandoned in favour of something altogether simpler and softer.

It is perhaps appropriate that a discussion of eleventh- and twelfth-century manuscripts should end with a mention of the Paris Psalter (Paris, Bibliothèque Nationale) (fig. 93). Although essentially another copy of the Utrecht Psalter, here the paintings are fully coloured, the figure style has moved away from the decorative patterning of Romanesque art, and only the iconography survives intact. This work clearly shows the changes in style that have taken place during the centuries, each phase of the development producing works of very high quality. The stage is now set for the gentler, more fluent style of English Gothic illumination.

Spain

There were two kinds of Christian in Spain during the ninth, tenth, and eleventh centuries; those in the north were free, constantly struggling to retain their independence against the Moslems of the south, but in addition there were many Christians living under Moslem rule. These people were known as Mozarabs. It is hardly surprising that Mozarabic art owes much to Arab influence, although one book of the late ninth century, the Bible of Monasterio della Cava dei Terreni, shows fairly strong influence of Carolingian art. It seems that, at first, they only used decorated initials. But only a handful of books datable before the end of the ninth century have survived.

The best-known early Spanish manuscripts are connected with Abbot Beatus of Liebana who lived during the eighth century. He is remembered chiefly for his Commentaries on the Revelations of St John the Divine – the Apocalypse – and his studies of the Prophecies of Daniel. These two books, which describe a mysterious world full of menace, were extremely popular among the troubled Christians in Spain, and form a basis for a large proportion of the illuminated books that survive today. There are no less than twenty-three illustrated copies of the Beatus Apocalypse and many of the scenes still retain their startling colours after a thousand years.

One such Apocalypse is the treasured possession of Gerona Cathedral. This is signed by the Presbyters Senior and Emeritus and by Ende 'Pintrix'. It is dated 975, and is abundantly enriched (figs. 41, 42 and 43) with scenes from the Life of Christ, Apocalyptic visions and numerous decorative birds and animals. Here is Mozarabic art at its very best, a work of dazzling originality with brilliantly coloured backgrounds of complementary hues. The illustration of the Fall of the Thunderbolts (fig. 43) endorses the instructive purpose of these books. It is a scene described in Revelations, Chapter iv, and the artist has closely followed the biblical text which tells of the twenty-four Elders 'arrayed in white garments; and on their heads crowns of gold'. The text, 'out of the throne proceed lightnings and voices of thunder', is written around the central medallion of the enthroned figure who points to the sealed book. St John himself is seen lying in a trance in the foreground of the painting. This didactic quality is very typical of Mozarabic art and in a sense foreshadows the French 'Bibles Moralisées' of the thirteenth century.

Other fine Mozarabic manuscripts, apart from the Beatus Apocalypses, include the Codex Vigilano or Albeldense and the Codex Emilianense, both now kept in the Escorial Library. They are books containing the acts of the Christian Councils and the latter is simply a copy of the Codex Vigilano. On the last page of the Codex Vigilano (fig. 45) figures of kings and queens are shown in separate panels and the bottom row contains

Vigila, the chief scribe, with his assistants Sarracino and Garsea. The very orderliness of the page and the grace of the draperies suggest some non-Spanish influence, and it has been thought that this manuscript was illustrated by a foreigner deeply imbued with Spanish feeling and technique. The Codex Emilianensis was begun the year in which the Vigilano was completed, and already the artists have returned to a purely Mozarabic style. The narrative paintings spread haphazardly over the whole page (fig. 44) and the human form is interpreted in a purely calligraphic way. The names of Velasco, Bishop Sisebuto and Notary Sisebuto replace the authors of the Codex Vigilano.

Unless we are lucky enough to know the date of a book, as in the case of the Gerona Beatus, the precise dating of Spanish manuscripts is difficult, but in general the eleventh- and twelfth-century illuminations show a gradual infiltration of trans-Pyrenean influence. A copy of the Beatus Apocalypse from Silos (London, British Museum) of *c* 1100 shows a more naturalistic interpretation of the subject-matter and the decorated initials have a southern-French character.

This bold, highly original manner of painting was more influential than one might expect. It had a strong impact on the neighbouring scriptoria of Southern France (the Apocalypse of St Sever, for instance) and on the art of Portugal, but it also spread further north and can be seen, rather suprisingly, in books made in the scriptorium of St Omer in Northern France. The Apocalyptic scenes in the Liber Floridus of Lambert of St Omer (Paris, Bibliothèque Nationale) reflect the Spanish love of brightly coloured backgrounds (fig. 78). The narrative is explained with the addition of texts, and surely the delightful dragons are of Spanish inspiration!

Italy

We must now turn from Spain, where the Christian monks had to devise a style of their own without the guidance of tradition and prototype, to Italy, a land with an almost unbroken heritage from Early Christian times and directly in contact with the Eastern Empire of Byzantium. In the days of the Ottonian Empire, Southern Italy was a bone of contention between German and Byzantine interests; the struggle was further complicated by the arrival of the Normans during the eleventh century. Stylistically, this is reflected in the art of the Benedictine Monastery of Montecassino, south of Rome. The abbot, Desiderius (1057–1085), had close connections with Constantinople; he sent there for mosaicists to decorate the church which he rebuilt, and commissioned Byzantine metalworkers to make a golden antependium decorated with scenes from the Life of St Benedict. How far the Eastern influences affected the work in the scriptorium at Montecassino can be seen in the Life of St Benedict and

St Maur (Rome, Vatican Library) written during the abbacy of Desiderius. It is illustrated with over a hundred small scenes from the lives of the saints. They are lively outline drawings filled in with colour washes and the debt to Byzantium is surprisingly superficial. Some of the initials show a knowledge of the Ottonian Sacramentary of Henry II, but there are no direct connections.

A phenomenon occurring in Southern Italy is the appearance of the Exultet Roll. This is a long strip of parchment containing the Easter Hymn which was sung by the priest during the Benediction of the Paschal Candle. The roll was illustrated with appropriate subjects for the faithful to look at as the manuscript was unrolled over the lectern. The illustrations are, of course, upside down to the reader. The Bari Roll, datable before 1028, is typical and shows the personification of Earth (fig. 48). These monumental figures were probably the artist's own creation and are without an apparent source of inspiration, but the borders decorated with medallions and the Beneventan script are reminiscent of the art of Montecassino.

It is clear from the style of wall-paintings in several churches in Rome that a series of large Bibles was written there. These 'Atlantic' Bibles often have full-page illustrations and their very scale allows broad brushwork and almost gives them the quality of fresco decoration. One such book is the Bible at Cividale del Friuli. For the late eleventh century this is a rather primitive style of painting. Folio 1 (fig. 50) shows scenes from the Creation; the narrative is ranged in horizontal bands and in each scene the most important figure is singled out against a darker strip of colour. Byzantine influence is apparent in the facial types but it has not stirred the spirit of the artist, who uses an unsophisticated repetition of forms (the two figures of God the Father are almost identical) and shows a sketchy unconcern for outline and drapery. A more refined example of these Atlantic Bibles is the Giant Bible (Munich, Staatsbibliothek) given to the Abbey of Hirsau by Emperor Henry IV about 1075. In general, Italian miniature painting is closely connected with the current trends in wall-painting, and this book has illustrations that are very like fresco cycles in Rome.

In spite of these Bibles, however, Central Italian manuscript illumination of the Romanesque period does not reach the glorious heights attained by the Anglo-Saxons or the Ottonian school. In contrast, it seems to be almost a minor art. A great number of books had simple ornamentation of the initials and can be classified into groups only after a painstaking examination of particular motifs.

In the north, however, the artists were more susceptible to extraneous influences than they were in the conservative cities of the south. The scriptoria, unlike those further south, were already active in the early part of the eleventh century, and such a book as the Sacramentary of Ivrea, *c* 1010, shows the acceptance of the German syle. At least four different hands are discernible in this manuscript; one artist uses realistic expressionism derived from a Carolingian manuscript like the Golden Psalter of St Gall, another shows closer affinities to the Ottonian style, and yet another gives his figures the mournful faces of Spain.

A late eleventh-century example of North Italian painting is the Missal (Milan, Biblioteca Ambrosiana) shown in figs. 51 and 52. The large 'V' of the words *Vere dignum* is faced by a rendering of the Crucifixion. The tight interlace at the corners of the framework, the 'Greek Key' and palmette decorations in the borders and the facial types suggest a wide variety of sources, characteristic of North Italian painting.

The Romanesque style of painting lasted a very long time in Italy, and in contrast to the rapid development elsewhere, there was no radical change until the emergence of a totally new kind of art in the frescoes at Assisi and the works of Giotto, heralding the Renaissance. A manuscript in Florence (Biblioteca Laurenziana) has initials and script that suggest an English twelfth-century provenance, but one page, left blank by the original artists, was decorated with scenes from the Trials of Job by an Italian artist of the thirteenth century. Poor Job (fig. 54), covered with sores, is sitting on the dunghill, watched over by his three friends. Minions of Satan taunt him from above and in the top corner we see the devastation of his house and family. The narrative effect is strong but it is hard to realize that this is contemporary with the sophisticated elegance of thirteenth-century France.

There was, however, an important if isolated group of artists in the court of Frederick II in Southern Italy and Sicily (*c* 1220–1250). Frederick himself was a great patron of all branches of the arts and was interested, perhaps for political reasons, in reviving the Antique, an interest that is reflected in the works of his sculptors and architects at Castel del Monte, near Capua. He also wrote a very detailed treatise on the art of falconry, and the illustrated copy in the Vatican of *c* 1250 has a series of delightful drawings executed with a vivid spontaneity and originality. A copy of Hippocrates' treatise on plants (Florence, Biblioteca Laurenziana) (fig. 53) reveals a mood far removed from the stylizations of Northern and Central Italy, and must surely originate from the circle of Frederick.

France

Any consideration of French Romanesque architecture requires the student to look at buildings in regional groups, each with its own peculiar characteristics. This approach is equally essential for the study of the illumination of the period. A country bordered by Germany, Italy, Spain and England, nations that produced such a diversity of styles in the eleventh and twelfth centuries, can hardly be expected to have a homogeneous national art. Moreover, the France of the eleventh and twelfth centuries was broken up into several separate feudal principalities. Until the establishment of the schools in Paris in the thirteenth century there are many differing trends in the art of manuscript illumination in France.

The arts seldom flourish during a time of stress, and after the decline of the Carolingian Empire, France suffered many years of invasion and pillage until the succession of the Capetians in the late tenth century. The monastic reforms promoted by Abbot Odilon (996–1048) and Abbot Hugh (1049–1109) of Cluny stressed the importance of the letter of the Benedictine Rule and enforced a stricter, more devout life in the monasteries. In this calmer atmosphere the scriptoria again began to produce fine work. The Carolingian heritage lies behind most of the Romanesque scriptoria of France, but for further inspiration the artists turned either to their neighbours or to books brought to their monasteries by travelling dignitaries of the Church.

In the south of France there is a strange, thin type of foliate interlace used in initials and borders. This purely decorative motif forms a link between many of the different scriptoria there and helps to tie them into a related group. A Beatus commentary on the Apocalypse from St Sever (Paris, Bibliothèque Nationale) is a French copy of the Spanish books. Here the Mozarabic influence is very strong, with motifs clearly drawn from Arabic inspiration. The figures are set against vivid backgrounds of red and yellow or of green and blue, and the precise handling gives the effect of sharply-cut enamels. St Sever is situated not far south of Bordeaux and the artist, Stephen Garcia, is a man deeply imbued with ideas from across the Pyrenees, but the initials are embellished with the long, emaciated tendrils of foliate interlace that originated in Albi and Toulouse.

In considering French painting, the importance of the Pilgrimage routes must not be underestimated. There were prescribed routes across France leading to the shrine of St James at Santiago de Compostela in north-western Spain. Along these routes important monasteries prospered; large churches were built for the use of the pilgrims and we can assume that certain voyagers left gifts rather than money as offerings. The Abbey of St Martial at Limoges was one such Pilgrimage church which no doubt received many visitors from foreign lands. Thus the books from its scriptorium reflect not only the south of France but also the works of the Ottonian masters. A great Bible from St Martial (Paris, Bibliothèque Nationale) dates from *c* 1100. It is the work of a very talented artist, with well balanced, clear compositions. The figures (fig. 73) stand in architectural settings rather like those of the Apocalypse of St

Sever and colour is carefully used to give the maximum decorative effect.

The southern-French forms spread a surprisingly long way north, to Anjou. The Angevin group of manuscripts comprises a Bible, a Psalter, and a Life of St Aubin from the abbey of St Aubin at Angers. These books are connected with the work of a certain Fulco, who was employed (1082–1108) to decorate the dependent priory of St Jean at Château Gontier. Allowing for the difference in scale and technique these works all seem to have been executed under the inspiration of the one man. The Life of St Aubin (Paris, Bibliothèque Nationale) has a heaviness that reflects the art of Poitou. The draperies (fig. 64) are solid and have sharply-cut folds that give the appearance of being made of a far stiffer material than mere cloth. These powerful and impressive illustrations, with their fine, strong colours, are the very essence of Romanesque painting.

Illumination in Burgundy at this time presents a rapid series of changes in style. Unfortunately most of the manuscripts from Cluny were lost when the abbey was destroyed during and after the French Revolution. The abbots of Cluny had close personal contacts with the German Empire and with Rome. Rhenish initials decorate the few books that remain, and in the paintings the figures are handled with a sympathy and care surpassed only in Byzantine books. Naturalistic use is made of the 'damp fold' convention and one is led to suspect the presence of Eastern artists. The St Hildefonsus manuscript (figs. 18 and 19), now at Parma, seems to originate from Cluny. It is, however, illustrated in a purely German style and again suggests that foreign artists were working at Cluny.

On the other hand, the early manuscripts of the new Cistercian monastery at Cîteaux show three very different styles following one another in rapid succession. The first two styles can even be seen in a single manuscript. This is the large four-volumed Bible known as the Bible of St Stephen Harding (Dijon, Bibliothèque Municipale), written and illustrated in the early years of the twelfth century. The first two volumes have elaborate historiated initials and coloured illustrations. St Stephen Harding, an Englishman from Sherborne, who became Abbot of Cîteaux in 1109, was no doubt responsible for the abrupt change in style. The new style (figs. 62 and 63) has all the spontaneity of the best English illuminations. Curious ugly faces and fat humorous figures find their closest parallels in such a book as the Shaftesbury Psalter (London, British Museum) which also comes from the West of England.

Historiated initials in a copy of St Gregory's Moralia in Job (Dijon, Bibliothèque Municipale) are equally English in character (figs. 65, 66 and 67) with light, bright colours and very animated figures. The initial 'R' which fills the whole page (fig. 67) is composed of two elegant athletes, one standing on the other's shoulders, about to attack a fine dragon.

The initial 'P' (fig. 66) has a complicated group of men fighting and animals biting each other.

Another Burgundian manuscript, almost comtemporary with the Bible of St Stephen Harding, is the Bible of St Bénigne (Dijon, Bibliothèque Municipale). This has initials, painted in strong colours on a gold ground, which contain scenes related to the text. The 'Q' at the beginning of the Gospel according to St Luke (fig. 68) has a half-human, half-symbolic figure seated at a desk while the 'H' at the beginning of the book of Exodus (fig. 69) is elaborated with a picture of Moses before Pharaoh. There is no lightness or pale colouring here, no subtle sense of humour, but heavy foliage and thick interlace. This book is also interesting because it includes some slightly later additions by a master at Cîteaux who painted a Madonna and Child and the Tree of Jesse in a copy of St Jerome's *Commentary on Isaiah* (Dijon, Bibliothèque Municipale) in a style that was quite new and full of naturalism and grace.

St Bernard, the severe Cistercian Abbot of Clairvaux, issued in 1134 his famous Condemnation of the pictorial representation of religious subjects. But his pronouncements had surprisingly few far-reaching effects on the illumination of manuscripts although some Cistercian books, notably the Bible of St Bernard (Troyes, Bibliothèque Municipale), abandoned every kind of narrative scene and all but the simplest colours. St Bernard's Bible is a masterpiece of elegant restraint with exquisite script and finely painted initials.

Between 986 and 1004 the Abbey of St Bertin at St Omer in north-eastern France was ruled by Abbot Odbert. The name Odbert suggests an Anglo-Saxon origin, and the books written during his abbacy show a very strong inclination towards the English style. The Gospels of St Bertin (Boulogne, Bibliothèque Municipale) must surely be the work of an Englishman; the drawing (figs. 55 and 56) has that same delightfully rapid technique, that feeling for movement and expression, found in the Benedictional of St Aethelwold. Odbert himself was also an artist and he has added his name to a Psalter now in Boulogne. Other books by him include an Aratus (Leyden), several Gospel Books, and a book of the Lives of St Bertin, St Folquin, St Silvin and St Winnoc (Boulogne, Bibliothèque Municipale), all saints connected with the Abbey of St Bertin. The illustration of St Bertin with his companions (figs. 57 and 58) reveals the strange character of Odbert. His portrayal of the human face has the hallmark of his style; these faces recur continually throughout his work and seem to have a constantly worried, quizzical expression. He has drawn his inspiration from a variety of sources and integrates his prototypes into a highly individual style. The architectural frame is a mixture of Ottonian and English motifs, while the decorative medallions contain contorted animals of Irish origin. Yet the figure style is curiously static with no suggestion of the wind-blown draperies of Anglo-Saxon art. Odbert shows an accomplished feeling for colour, which he uses with good decorative results.

The effect of the Norman Conquest on English illumination has already been considered. In Normandy, the Conquest heralds the birth of the true Romanesque style, although the exact role played by England is rather complex. In fact, the English influence soon fades, and new ideas give rise to quite individual styles at places like the Mont St Michel. We have seen that the stylistic developments can be traced at Canterbury in its four copies of the Utrecht Psalter. Similarly there are three copies of the Life of St Amand from the Abbey of St Amand at Valenciennes (now in the Library at Valenciennes).

The first of these dates from the end of the eleventh century and sets the pattern for the other two. Forty scenes from the Life of the Saint are spaced among the text and handled in a rather simple, painterly manner. The second Life (figs. 60 and 61) is much more stylized. It is the work of an assured artist of the mid-twelfth century, who at times uses a strange drapery convention. He cuts off a whole area of the drapery with a thick line and inside this he models the shape beneath with paint (fig. 61). This is a technique that brings to mind the art of enamels and stained glass. We must not forget that this particular area of north-eastern France and the valley of the river Meuse were renowned for their wonderful metalwork, both in enamel and in bronze, and this may well have influenced the illuminators. The third Life of St Amand (fig. 70), produced at the end of the twelfth century, marks the culmination of the Romanesque style at St Amand. It has only seven illustrations, but each is of extremely high quality. The choice of colours – old rose, brilliant yellows, blues and purples – is magnificent and the elegance and sophistication foreshadow the advent of the Gothic style.

Also from St Amand comes a Bible in five volumes (Valenciennes, Bibliothèque Municipale). Each volume opens with a full-page initial set against a carpet of foliage decoration. The 'A' that opens volume four (fig. 71) is signed by Savalo, Monk of St Amand. The initial is made up of an elaborate arrangement of dragons' bodies set against a background of foliage, with animals and human beings clambering about among the branches. The tortuous delicacy of the page is again reminiscent of the fine chasing of metalled surfaces.

The influence of England in this area does not end with the eleventh century. From Liessies, there are two Evangelist portraits from a Gospel Book (Avesnes, Société Archéologique) that have very close affinities with the English Lambeth Bible. The curious drapery conventions are very similar, although the faces resemble those in books from St Amand more closely. Although the Avesnes Leaves are still essentially Romanesque in style, it is significant that they should show close artistic connections with England. It is in this milieu that the new Gothic style will be born.

Gothic Manuscript Illumination

The Transition from Romanesque to Gothic

If we compare a twelfth-century manuscript like the third Life of St Amand (fig. 70) with a mid-thirteenth-century book such as the Psalter of St Louis (fig. 75), we can see that a tremendous change in style has taken place during the first half of the thirteenth century. The complete change in attitude cannot be traced along one simple route. Before one can assess the new style in its entirety, half a century of complex ideas and contradictions must be disentangled.

To some extent the emergence of the new style is due in France, as in England, to fresh contact with the Byzantine Empire, either through Sicily or direct from Constantinople itself. A new naturalism is particularly noticeable in a book such as the Souvigny Bible (Paris, Bibliothèque Nationale), where the scenes are permeated with a new sense of form and composition. The question of where this new movement first appeared is complicated by the fact that a group of books which were probably written in France during the exile of St Thomas Becket was given to Canterbury. A monk of Canterbury, Manerius, was the scribe of a three-volumed Bible (Paris, Bibliothèque Ste Geneviève). The Bible of St André au Bois (Boulogne, Bibliothèque Municipale) has initials filled with fighting men of extraordinary violence (fig. 59). These two books along with several others can all be grouped together because of the style of their initials. All are decorated with thick acanthus foliage emerging from an ordered pattern of stems, and all have powerful colouring.

In these early transitional books the importance of Mosan metalwork must again be stressed. Many of the small bronze statuettes of the second half of the twelfth century have remarkably naturalistic draperies with the fabric drawn back from the knees in a series of parallel folds. The panels on the Klosterneuburg Altarpiece, made by Nicholas of Verdun in 1181, have figures of a style closely reflected in a book such as the Ingeborg Psalter (Chantilly, Musée Condé). This Psalter (fig. 82) was written for the Danish queen of Philip Augustus, King of France, and was probably made *c* 1200. The paintings have taken on the metallic quality of their prototypes and the draperies have the swinging, horizontal folds of the work of Nicholas of Verdun. This style occurs again in another medium in some of the stone figures at Reims.

The sketchbook of Villard d'Honnecourt does not properly come within the scope of this introduction to manuscript illumination, but it should be mentioned at this point. Architectural designs must have been carried from one centre to another in pattern books. Unfortunately, these were not considered as items of importance and were destroyed by later generations. However, the sketchbook of Villard has survived and tells us a great deal about the spread of artistic ideas. He drew buttresses, rose windows, and ground plans primarily from the point of view of an architect. But it is most likely that painters also used sketchbooks, and in any case, we eventually find that Gothic painters, masons and metalworkers all shared the same basic repertory of forms. Quite apart from drawing, the new style was considerably influenced by the art of stained glass. The area of glass in Romanesque churches was comparatively small, and decoration principally took the form of wall-painting, to which large areas could be devoted. But as the architects perfected the technique of stone vaulting they were able to lighten the load with the use of flying buttresses and make far larger window openings. These were filled with stained glass. This new medium allowed great scope for pictorial artists, who, in their turn, influenced the illuminators of manuscripts.

France

It is no accident that the new style was born in France. The University of Paris was the intellectual centre of Europe throughout the thirteenth century, and from the time of St Louis (1226–*c* 1270) the French court became increasingly important. Students and scholars from all over the continent flocked to Paris to learn and to discuss scholarly matters. Knights returning from the Crusades introduced Eastern theory and science. With the ascendancy of the university, the importance of monasteries as centres of illumination declined. Commercial guilds were founded and books were produced for private ownership. Large ceremonial books became less common and we must follow the stylistic developments principally in Psalters, which the highborn laity made their own. Eventually the Psalter gave way to even smaller Books of Hours, but the former was more popular during the thirteenth century.

The development in painting during the first half of the century can be followed in a succession of Psalters written for the royal house at Paris. The first of this group has already been mentioned; it is the Ingeborg Psalter (Chantilly, Musée Condé) written for the queen of Philip Augustus. Secondly, there is the Psalter of Blanche of Castile, a book probably brought from York by her husband Louis. It seems unlikely that either of these books was written in Paris; the Ingeborg Psalter has distinctly Mosan characteristics and that of Blanche of Castile has many English features. In contrast, a Psalter written *c* 1230, for the Norwegian princess, Christine, seems to have been written in Paris. Originating in Paris at the same date is another Psalter that has always been connected with the name of Blanche of Castile (Paris, Bibliothèque de l'Arsenal). It shows (fig. 74) scenes enclosed in medallions, interlocking like panels of stained glass. A reminder of the Ingeborg style persists in the sculptural folds of the Madonna's drapery, but this mannerism is abandoned in the smaller figures. Rich, fleshy acanthus foliage in the border is still reminiscent of late-twelfth-century Bibles, with its curled edges and the curious method of indicating a fold in the leaf by a series of white dots. Romanesque details are entirely absent in a Psalter written C 1250 (Paris, Bibliothèque Nationale). Here (fig. 76) the scenes, set beneath trilobate architraves, are richly coloured. The figures, set against a ground of patterned gold, are treated with a new simplicity; drapery conventions give way to a new interest in soft vertical folds and uncluttered outlines.

These last two Psalters set the stage for the most lavish psalter of them all: the Psalter of St Louis (Paris, Bibliothèque Nationale). This was made between 1253 and the king's death in 1270. It has seventy-eight full-page illustrations of scenes from the Old Testament. The book is closely connected with St Louis' other artistic activities, as the architectural settings are exact copies of details in the Sainte Chapelle, built by his architect Pierre de Montreuil. Painted in rich colours, the figures are set against a background of shimmering gold that seems to bathe them in glorious sunlight. They are extremely elegant in design with small heads and tall thin bodies that move with an easy grace. This is above all an 'édition de luxe', adjudged worthy of the great king.

The typology of the Bible Moralisée was a product of the thirteenth-century Dominican scholar Hugh of St Cher. It contains scenes from the Bible juxtaposed with scenes of moral significance. Several copies of this great work were made, the most important being the Bible Moralisée de St Louis (Paris, Bibliothèque Nationale, London, British Museum, and Oxford, Bodleian). In this the texts are supported by the use of illustrations and each biblical event is shown with its moralizing counterpart. The pages seem like stained glass transposed onto parchment. Each folio (fig. 84) has medallions arranged in vertical rows of four with intervening strips of text replacing the mullions of the windows. The colours have the luminosity achieved in stained glass and the figures are drawn with strong outlines that remind us of the leads. Sometimes the actual quality varies but the artists must be to some degree excused as the whole book contained over five thousand medallions.

Towards the end of the thirteenth century, we see the emergence of the manuscript illuminator as a distinct artistic personality. More than one documentary reference is made to a Master Honoré of the Rue Boutebrie in Paris. His name occurs in the accounts books of the king and in one manuscript, Decretals of Gratian (Tours, Bibliothèque Municipale). On the basis of stylistic comparison other books can be attributed to Master Honoré, notably the Breviary of Philippe le Bel (Paris, Bibliothèque Nationale). Certainly another book written for the royal house, this contains historiated initials and one full-page illustration of scenes from the Life of David (fig. 79). The narrative is easy to follow, with the names of the principal characters written below the figures. This work marks the culmination of the trends embarked upon during the earlier part of the century. The scenes are full of life and the movement of the figures is clearly shown beneath the draperies. The artist still retains the patterned backgrounds, but in the lower scene he has introduced hills scattered with trees to suggest a naturalistic setting.

Jean Pucelle, who worked in Paris during the second quarter of the fourteenth century, was another professional illuminator like Master Honoré. Pucelle was undoubtedly the artist of the Belleville Breviary and the Billyng Bible (both in the Bibliothèque Nationale, Paris), and his hand can also be traced in several other Books of Hours. This artist used the marginal decorations that were so popular in the north of France and in England, filling margins with rustic scenes borrowed from everyday life. Butterflies and snails cling to ripening tendrils of peas, and dragonflies glide among the foliage while the farmer gathers the harvest. His new interest in nature is perfectly shown in the Labours of the Months where the usual scenes, chopping wood or sowing crops, are replaced by a tree whose branches show the change in foliage at different times of the year. Although the successor of Master Honoré, and essentially a Parisian artist, Jean Pucelle is important because he also shows a knowledge of Italian painting. The Papal court moved from Rome to Avignon in 1309, and the great Sienese artist, Simone Martini, was working there in the latter part of his life. Despite a somewhat superficial understanding of the Italian manner, Pucelle could not yet grasp the plastic treatment of volumes and space. For a full mastery of these lessons from Italy, we must wait for another generation, whose achievements are generally referred to under the heading of the International Gothic Style.

England

In the discussion of English Romanesque manuscripts, we left the development of illumination at the threshold of a new era. Signs of a change had become evident in a work such as the Winchester Bible, *c* 1170, but there is no particular work produced in the next fifty years which can be called a truly Gothic manuscript. The period of transition is a protracted process of experiment and change. The close stylistic similarities between manuscripts written in France and in England have already been mentioned. Their destination can often be determined by the inclusion or exclusion of particular saints in the Calendar, but usually even this does not tell us much about the nationality of the artist, as there were certainly French artists working in English scriptoria and Englishmen working in France. The Paris copy of the Utrecht Psalter (fig. 93) seems to be a case in point.

At the close of the twelfth century, the fashion for great Bibles destined for ceremonial use gives way to smaller works for theological study and Psalters for the private devotions of lay people. With the change in scale of the books, the quality of the painting tended to become more delicate and minute. However, monastic scriptoria survived longer in England than in France and there was major activity at St Albans and Winchester at least until the middle of the thirteenth century.

The transitional period is well illustrated in a work such as the Huntingfield Psalter (New York, Pierpont Morgan Library). A book which shows rather similar trends is the Psalter at Imola (figs. 88 and 89). The beginning of the first Psalm is shown on a two-page opening with the initial 'B' of 'Beatus' facing a decorated page with the first verse of the Psalm. The 'B' contains the Dream of Jesse. A calm, balanced orderliness pervades the illustration, with kings and prophets ranged symmetrically at the interstices of the initial and the border enriched by stories from the Life of David. The arrangement of the text on a coloured ground was very popular at this date and has a sober beauty.

A Bible (London, British Museum) was written for Robert de Bello, Abbot of Canterbury from 1224 to 1253. It is larger than most books of this date and has a large initial at the beginning of the Book of Genesis (fig. 92) filled with scenes from the Creation. To make room for scenes of the Original Sin, the initial 'I' has been extended along the bottom into an 'L' shape, allowing room for only one column of text. Each scene is contained within a medallion as in the contemporary French books, but the foliate projections from the edge of the initial are a new feature and will be taken to far greater lengths in later books.

Some of the best books of the second quarter of this century are associated with the shadowy figure of W. de Brailes. Only the artist's name is known. Where he came from, whether he was a monastic or secular ecclesiastic, a travelling artist or based in one scriptorium, are questions to which answers can be only speculative. His name occurs in two manuscripts and several others are attributed on stylistic grounds. W. de Brailes has all the abilities of a good story-teller. He is able to translate the ideas of his vivid imagination into lively painted stories. Having a remarkable knowledge of the details of biblical events he did not hesitate to put it to work in his illuminations. The leaves of a Psalter (Cambridge, Fitzwilliam Museum) contain one instance of W. de Brailes' autograph; it is charmingly shown on a little figure singled out from the Damned in the Last Judgement, apparently in hope of having his labours rewarded by Salvation.

A far more tangible personality is Matthew Paris. Born *c* 1200, Paris entered the Monastery of St Albans in 1217, and is known to have had contact with the king and other noblemen. In 1235, he was appointed historiographer to the Abbey of St Albans and composed two chronicles now divided between the British Museum and Corpus Christi College, Cambridge. One of the separate pages which are bound into the Chronicles has a drawing of the Madonna and Child. This famous leaf (fig. 97), showing Paris himself prostrated at the feet of the Madonna, is a monumental work of art. Paris' qualities as a draughtsman are amply displayed, giving the drawing a firm, expressive form. The figures have a regal poise but come to life with the lively handling of the draperies, tinted with pale washes of colour. The text of the Chronicle is richly illustrated with relevant scenes sketched in the margins and at the foot of the pages, giving us an instructive account of historical events between 1230 and 1251. Not all the illustrations, in a work of such magnitude, are by the Master himself, but a consistency of subject-matter suggests that Matthew Paris was responsible for the design of the whole series.

The influence of Matthew Paris is strongly felt in a group of Apocalypses that originate from St Albans. A large group of this type from Romanesque Spain has already been mentioned, but the sudden popularity of the Apocalypse in mid-thirteenth-century England is difficult to explain. Among the best is the one in Trinity College, Cambridge, which is prefaced by scenes from the Life of St John. Another interesting Apocalypse (fig. 98) was commissioned from St Albans by an English nobleman. French was the accepted language of the aristocrat and accordingly this book is in that tongue, and, by chance, preserved not in England but in the French capital (Bibliothèque Nationale). It has ninety-two illustrations at the top of the pages of text, and is again prefaced with full-page scenes arranged in two tiers, from the Life of St John. The illustrations, like those in the Chronicles, are executed in pen and ink with washes of colour. This fondness for outline drawing, so noticeable at Anglo-Saxon Winchester, still persists into the Gothic era. Scenes are filled with animated figures, but now the movement of the characters is expressed in more solid forms, with shadows helping to mould the body.

As patronage changed, the choice of subjects also changed. Representations of the Madonna and Child are comparatively rare in Romanesque books, but with the rise of a gentler, more human approach, paintings of the Virgin and Child are included in many Psalters. The Matthew Paris drawing has already been mentioned. A touching example also occurs in the Amesbury Psalter (Oxford, All Souls College) where a nun, probably the owner of the book, is seen at the feet of the Madonna who suckles her Child. The nun appears again at the feet of Christ in Majesty (fig. 96), where the setting is arranged with elaborate architectural details. The Amesbury Psalter sums up the achievements of the mid-thirteenth century. A skilful choice of rich colours reverberates against a golden background, elegant willowy figures sway in delicate curves, and yet the draperies retain a nervous energy that suggests intense devotion.

In general, the illumination of the latter half of the thirteenth century reaffirms its connections with France. This is particularly evident in a book like the Tenison Psalter (London, British Museum) which was intended for no less a person than a son of King Edward I. The illustrations are of minute proportions set inside a large area of patterned background, and the scenes have become exquisitely elegant. The margins of the pages are decorated with a border containing birds and animals and strange little grotesques as well as scenes from everyday life. Margin decorations were to become one of the hallmarks of the East Anglian school. From about 1300, for reasons that are not at all easy to understand, the school of East Anglia became increasingly important and it is in this area that we can trace the important stylistic developments of the next thirty or forty years.

From a group of Psalters of very high quality, the Ormesby Psalter (Oxford, Bodleian) and the Gorleston Psalter (London, British Museum) can be singled out. Here the traditional biblical scenes are arranged alongside all kinds of fantastic and secular images. The margins are filled with butterflies and ladybirds, with centaurs and dragons, monkeys and men. Babewyn is the name given to these marginalia and, although in its strictest sense it derives from the Italian word for baboon, it is now given to all kinds of grotesques. Gradually this emphasis on margin decoration begins to outweigh the narrative content of the Psalters. For example, in the Gorleston Psalter, which is a few years later than the Ormesby Psalter, preoccupation with the secular decoration becomes paramount. The style of this work is more humorous and even satirical – the artists show rabbits conducting a funeral! This is a far cry from the twelfth-century bestiaries intended for instruction.

These marginalia were popular on both sides of the Channel and abound in manuscripts of this date from north-eastern France and the Low Countries, but the more serious features of these books are also worthy of comment. We have seen that in France Jean Pucelle showed some knowledge of the great pictorial developments in Italy at a surprisingly early date. The speed at which artistic influence spread from one country to another must not be underestimated, for a parallel knowledge of Italian painting appears in England at this time. There is no certain evidence that Italians were working in England, but if one examines the paintings it becomes clear that English artists must have known the works of the great Italian masters. The Ormesby Psalter was substantially complete before 1325 but some additions were made at about this date, and it is here that the Italian influence is apparent. A real attempt is made to gain depth in the picture plane and the figures are given a certain weight. This Italianism is even more noticeable in slightly later books like the Douai Psalter (now badly damaged) and the Psalter of St Omer (London, British Museum). The artists of these books interpreted the Italian treatment of drapery forms in much the same way as did Jean Pucelle, using heavy swinging folds of soft materials. The Psalter of Robert de Lisle (London, British Museum) is particularly interesting as it shows the later stage of the East Anglian school as well as the style of some twenty-five years earlier. In the later illustrations of this book the artist, beginning to understand perspective, is able to crowd his figures in a group fairly satisfactorily.

However, this particular phase of Italian influence was inconclusive in England. In the Psalter written in East Anglia *c* 1340, for Sir Geoffrey Luttrell of Irnham in Lincolnshire, already we see it fading. Figures become flatter again and are described by linear rhythms. The Luttrell Psalter is not unfairly described as the show-piece of the East Anglian school in its decadence. The fresh originality gives way to a harder, more mechanical technique, but this book contains a celebrated series of farmers at work, scenes full of interest for the social historian even though the actual handling is coarse and rather heavy.

Queen Mary's Psalter (London, British Museum) is one of the finest English Gothic manuscripts. Although not a product of the East Anglian school, the artist owes something to their example. It is prefaced by sixty-six scenes from the Old Testament, and has other full-page illustrations and countless margin decorations of the highest quality. If, as seems probable, this book is the work of one artist alone, then it is even more remarkable. Its characteristics are those of the English school – fine outline drawings and thin washes of delicate colour.

The Black Death (1348–1349) was probably responsible for the somewhat meagre output of English manuscripts between *c* 1350 and 1370. However, there was no complete break and a small number of manuscripts helped to fill the gap. The most interesting of these is the Egerton Genesis (London, British Museum) which perhaps shows the only episode in the history of English manuscript illumination where the artist, or artists, made any serious attempt to come to terms with the deeper significance of the Renaissance ideas that were being formulated in Italy. The actual subject-matter of this book has no English prototypes and although the illustrations are drawn in characteristic English outlines, the style must be partially derived from Italy.

The hand of the master of the Egerton Genesis can be seen in two pages of the Fitzwarin Hours (Paris, Bibliothèque Nationale), although the rest of the book is far more English in character. The most striking feature of the Fitzwarin Hours is the introduction of fantastic pinnacles in the architectural settings and in the framework of the miniatures.

These same fantasies of architecture, structures that could never have been built, form the link with an important group of books written for Humphrey de Bohun, Earl of Leicester. His death is recorded in 1373, providing an approximate date for the group, but his family continued the patronage. The Psalter in Brescia may be loosely connected with this group of works. English tradition survives strongly in the lay-out of the page (fig. 94), but the extraneous animals and grotesques are far less prominent. By now we begin to see a reaffirmation of the influence of France. During the next decade other new ideas are introduced into English miniature, and manuscripts in England, as elsewhere, form a part of the European International Style.

Germany

The development of the Gothic style in Germany was not centralized as it was in France. There was no stabilizing influence comparable to the royal house in Paris, and monastic scriptoria survived far longer. In this atmosphere, different parts of the country continued to develop their own individual ideas. If only for this reason, it seems more profitable, in discussing Gothic painting in this region, to disregard the present-day boundaries of Germany and to consider Central European painting as a whole. In the space of a short introduction, only a limited survey can be made of the principal developments in this very large area.

Manuscripts of the first half of the thirteenth century in Germany present a special problem for classification. Are they Romanesque or Gothic? On balance they should be grouped with the Gothic works, as they present another aspect of the importance of Byzantium in the formation of the new style. The Berthold Missal (New York, Pierpont Morgan Library) from Weingarten, was written soon after 1200 and clearly shows fresh ideas. Instead of the habitual line-drawings of the late twelfth century, we have paintings in rich, strong colours. The debt to Byzantine examples is paramount, and a competent narrative ability is combined with a good sense of composition. The figures are given the qualities of sculpture, and again one is reminded of the art of metalwork.

One of the striking features of this second wave of influence from the East is that it soon becomes submerged beneath the national characteristics of the artists. This is particularly noticeable in the Psalters written for Landgraf Hermann of Thuringia during the first decades of the thirteenth century. Among these is the Psalter of St Elizabeth now at Cividale (figs. 106 and 107). This is a sumptuous book illustrated in rich reds, blues and golds, containing isolated events from the Old Testament as well as scenes from the Life of Christ. Again the Byzantine element is clearly apparent in the faces and in the weightiness of the figures, but the draperies are sharp and angular, broken up into a series of jagged, horizontal folds. This particular mannerism seems to have originated in the north of Germany, but it soon spread south and east to Bavaria, Austria and Bohemia. It became more and more exaggerated as we see in a Psalter from the Tyrol (New York, Pierpont Morgan Library). The illustration shown in fig. 102 is dominated by a frenzy of zigzag folds. Later this feature governs the whole spirit of the illuminations and lends the paintings a nervous, excited expressionism that reminds us of those great Evangelist portraits of the Ottonian age. It reaches its climax in books like the Mainz Gospels (Munich, Staatsbibliothek) and the Bonmont Psalter (Besançon, Bibliothèque Municipale). However, it is in works such as these that we also see the first signs of influence from France. The Bonmont Psalter has purely French initials with Gothic foliage.

How the French style came to Germany at this date, *c* 1250, is difficult to assess, but it must be attributed partly to the monastic orders of the Cistercians and Dominicans. Gradually it spread eastwards and reached Bohemia before 1300. Small Books of Hours never really came into fashion in Germany, so there are rarely direct copies of subject-matter from French books. It is in legal textbooks, chronicles and secular works that we first see the influence of the French style.

One of the finest secular books of the Middle Ages is the Minnesänger Manuscript of the Manesse family (Heidelberg, University Library). This is a collection of paintings of poets, lovers and troubadours made for Rudger Manesse von Maneck of Zurich, who died in 1304, and it was completed by his son Johannes. Among the subjects we find King Wenzel of Bohemia (1278–1305), the poet Wolfram von Eschenbach (1170–1220) and Heinrich Frauenlob conducting his orchestra (fig. 100). Suddenly we have emerged into a new world of delicate court art. Careful attention is paid to details of costume; a cape of ermine is draped over the shoulders of the conductor and fur trimmings edge the coat of the central musician. The whole book is filled with lively, topical narrative and is a supremely decorative work of art.

A copy of Wolfram von Eschenbach's poem, *Willehalm von Oranse*, was made in 1334 for Landgraf Henry II, and used to be one of the treasured possessions of the library at Cassel. The manuscript was tragically lost during the Second World War, but photographs survive to bear witness to its beauty. Artistically the paintings were of a higher quality than the Minnesänger manuscript and revealed an artist of great stature. He probably came from Cologne, and his hand can be seen again in the Gradual of Wettingen (Aarau, Kantonsbibliothek) where the elegant figures seem to be weighed down with heavy, flowing draperies. One wonders if the artist knew the work of Jean Pucelle.

Bohemia

Before the accession of the Luxembourg dynasty (1311), the native art of Bohemia clearly shows the different foreign influences from which it draws its inspiration. From the north we see the typical agitated draperies of the Saxon-Thuringian school, from Venice in the south come strong traces of Byzantium and of Italy, and from the west comes French influence that added refinement to the whole. After the accession of John of Luxembourg, these latter influences become more prominent. Commissions from the royal house at Prague in the early fourteenth century include books modelled on Franciscan manuscripts, and it is these works which initiate the fine tradition of Bohemian manuscript illumination that continues into the International Gothic period of the early fifteenth century.

The Passional of Abbess Kunigunda (Prague, University Library) was written for Kunigunda, daughter of the King of Bohemia. The princess died in 1321 and the book must have been written and illustrated before this date. The Passional is unfinished, but the illustrations are of the finest quality. They include the moving scene of Christ taking leave of His Mother (fig. 109). Intense, deep emotion binds the two together and seems to exclude the onlooker. The group is enclosed in a single outline and the vertical lines of the drapery lead the eye towards the two expressive heads. Stylistically the painting reflects something of the art of France, an influence to be seen again in the Velislav Bible (Prague, National Library) which was illustrated some twenty years later. The typology of this Picture Bible is based on books of the Fransciscan order; it is a comparatively large book with over seven hundred illustrations accompanied by an explanatory text. It was made for Velislav, who was later to become Chancellor to Emperor Charles IV. The linear qualities of the Passional are developed further in this manuscript (fig. 110), where the scenes are drawn in pen and ink and are only slightly coloured.

In 1348, Charles IV founded the great University of Prague and thus opened the gates of Bohemia to foreign artists and craftsmen who flocked to Prague. It was in this international atmosphere that the new unified style was to be created.

Italy

At a time when Matthew Paris and Master Honoré were distinguishing the art of manuscript illumination in England and France, illuminators in Italy were still struggling for an individual style. Today, Italian manuscript illumination of the late thirteenth century is still regarded as an essentially minor art, totally overshadowed by the achievements of Cimabue, Giotto and Duccio. This fact is in itself significant, and it is important to remember that in Italy new developments can invariably be traced to panel-paintings and frescoes whereas in the north the first advances are made in illuminated books.

Bologna is one of the oldest and most celebrated university cities, and it is here that we find the first centre of Gothic book decoration. A real workshop seems to have existed here, producing not only secular textbooks and books for theological instruction, but also service books for ecclesiastical foundations. Legal codices were numerous; a good example can be seen in the illustrated Book of Civil Law (Turin, Biblioteca Nazionale) which contains scenes in brilliant colours. In fig. 114, which shows Justice at work, the figures are handled with a strong plasticity, no doubt due to the omnipresent influence of Giotto, and the scenes are endowed with a vibrant vitality.

The Bolognese school, with its firm construction of figures and sober use of decoration, finds its greatest exponent in Niccolo da Giacomo. This artist, working during the second half of the fourteenth century, was head of a large workshop and a number of manuscripts contain his signature. Niccolo da Giacomo was a highly gifted individualist. The copy of Lucan's *Pharsalia* (Milan, Biblioteca Trivulziana) (fig. 115) is typical of his best work and shows many of his characteristic traits. No ideal beauty restrains him; the faces have curiously livid complexions; gaudy colours and a showy superficiality emphasize the secular character of the master.

Florence, more than any other city, shows the subordination of manuscript illumination to the more monumental forms of art. Reflections of the paintings of Cimabue can be seen in the large choir books of San Marco, and Pacino da Buonaguida based both his iconography and his style on that of Giotto. His works are crude and rather heavy, almost as if he was unwilling to reduce the scale of his prototypes to the minute decorations of books. The *Biadaiolo* (Florence, Biblioteca Laurenziana) is a sort of 'mirror of life' and contains scenes relating to everyday events. It was composed by a Florentine grain-merchant as a kind of diary. Fig. 124 shows the Colle di Valdelsa with asses being driven out of the town. Those on the left are going unladen towards Florence where the prices of grain were low, the others are carrying the grain to Pisa where a better price could be obtained. The tale is simply told with a few figures; it is colourful and essentially a popular manuscript, yet a masterpiece in its own way.

Early Gothic manuscripts of Siena show connections with the scriptoria of Bologna, but the style is modified under the influence of the great Duccio. The greatest illuminator of the Sienese School was undoubtedly Simone Martini. Only one page remains to bear witness to his skill as an illuminator. This is the frontispiece to a copy of Virgil that belonged to Petrarch (Milan, Biblioteca Ambrosiana). Simone made friends with Petrarch during his prolonged sojourn at Avignon and no doubt the humanistic character of the illustration is due to Petrarch's own instructions. The style of the painting shows a wonderful fusion of the linear rythmns that Simone had learnt in France and the brilliant colours of Italy's Byzantine tradition. In some ways, Simone was really an artist ahead of his time. He died at Avignon in 1344, and his immediate influence is hard to assess, but the art of Simone was certainly a moving force in the formation of the International Style a generation later, and it was at that time that the Sienese regarded him as their greatest artist.

In Venice and Milan the most important manuscripts do not appear until the closing stages of the fourteenth century, and it seems more profitable to discuss these in the later entry on the International Gothic Style.

The International Gothic Style

The birth of an international movement in art is often the natural outcome of close political ties between nations. In 1348, Charles IV of Bohemia became Emperor of Germany. His mother was French, he had been educated in France, and had married a French princess. The ascendancy of Prague as an international centre of culture dates from this period, and the University, based on those at Paris and Bologna, welcomed the Italian humanists Rienzo and Petrarch. Among the artists summoned by the Emperor were the mason Matthieu d'Arras to work on the cathedral of Prague, Johannes Gallicus, a goldsmith, and Tommaso da Modena, an Italian painter. Matthieu d'Arras had earlier been employed by the papal court at Avignon. In 1382, Anne of Bohemia became the wife of Richard II and there is ample evidence to show that she brought Bohemian artists with her to England. The cosmopolitan employment of artists can also be seen in the building of Milan Cathedral where French and German architects co-operated with Lombards at the request of the Visconti family. One fascinating aspect of the International Gothic Style is that no one city, or even country, can claim sole rights of origin. It seems to have been a movement that developed simultaneously in several places at once, presumably at the confluence of different ideas.

The International Style is characterized by a deeper understanding, a new appreciation of nature. The artists conceive new ideals of beauty and fill their pages with wonderfully accurate details. It is essentially an art destined for the aristocrat with his worldly pleasures, his fine horses and fairytale castles reflected in the paintings. However, this is no empty superficiality, for the religious paintings are imbued with a deeply devotional mysticism.

France

Paris, a supremely important cultural centre, also attracted artists from abroad. There were certainly Italians working there during the later years of the fourteenth century, notably Zenobo da Firenze, who illuminated a Book of Hours for Charles, king of Navarre, and the artists who gathered around the Italian poetess Christine de Pisan. The main stream of immigrants, however, came from the north. Among them came Jean Bondol, an artist born in Bruges and working in Paris from 1368 to 1381. This man is usually thought to be the same artist as the 'Maître de Boquetaux,' so called because of his use of small clumps of trees. The page illustrated (fig. 81) from St Augustine's *De Civitate Dei* (Paris, Bibliothèque Nationale) does not show his characteristic landscapes but it reveals a new understanding and a sense of the volume of the human figure.

As a centre of manuscript illumination the importance of Paris waned temporarily in face of the great patronage of the Dukes of Burgundy. In 1361, the lands of Burgundy reverted to the French crown and were given by the king to his son Philip the Bold, brother of the future king Charles V. This duke married Margaret, daughter of the Count of Flanders, and in 1384 he inherited the whole of Flanders. Flemish sculptors, painters and goldsmiths flocked to his court at Dijon, among them Claus Sluter, the sculptor of the famous doorway at the Chartreuse de Champmol and the Puits de Moïse.

Philip the Bold's younger brother, Jean, duc de Berry, was also a great patron and was very closely concerned with the production of his books. He often had extra scenes painted into them, and judging from the great number of unfinished books from his library we must assume that he often did not have the patience to await their completion! A real connoisseur, he vied with his brother Philip the Bold for the employment of the very finest artists.

The Très Belles Heures in Brussels (Bibliothèque Royale) was illustrated by a Fleming, Jacquemart de Hesdin, who was court painter to the Duc de Berry in 1402. The paintings include an exquisitely beautiful Madonna and Child (fig. 129). Against a background of a choir of angels, the Madonna is sitting on a high-sided throne as she suckles the Child, who fidgets impatiently on her knees. This is a Madonna full of earthly grace and humanity, a touching scene of mother and child. The draperies fall to the ground and over the chair in soft, heavy folds. The 'International' character can be seen in the small mouth and the almond-shaped eyes typical of Sienese painting and in the long slim fingers characteristic of Bohemia. The grace and serenity of the page is enhanced by a restrained border with little birds and butterflies resting on the flowered foliage.

Jacquemart de Hesdin disappeared from court circles in 1409 and his place was taken by three brothers–Pol, Jean and Herman de Limbourg. Their masterpiece was, of course, the Très Riches Heures du Duc de Berry (Chantilly, Musée Condé). The Calendar that prefaces the Hours is shown in a semicircle at the top of each of the twelve pages and is embellished with signs of the Zodiac set against a starry sky. The usual Labours of the Months are replaced by scenes of the Duke himself, going about his courtly pursuits. December shows a stag hunt, the hounds at the kill before a wooded thicket, and January (fig. 134) shows the noble Duke entertaining his friends. A lavish feast is spread before them, wine flows from golden ewers and the host bids his guests draw near. All the scenes have this intriguing quality of intimate detail. Court costumes and the manners of the rich can be minutely studied.

The most remarkable feature of this beautiful book is the almost incredible advance made in the development of landscape painting. Suddenly we have great vistas reaching into the distance; castles and trees are drawn with loving care and the sky pales as it touches the horizon. There is a new, if not complete, understanding of pictorial perspective, which must derive from Italy. A pervasive Italianism is evident in the architectural settings, with actual details taken from the Cathedral of Milan. There is no reason to think that the de Limbourg brothers travelled to Italy, but they must have had close contacts with the Italian artists working in Paris before they came to the court of Jean, Duc de Berry. Such fine examples of landscape-painting were not to be seen again until the emergence of such great Flemish masters as Jan van Eyck.

In fact, the van Eycks may well have known the work of the de Limbourg brothers, even if they did not know the artists themselves. The Très Belles Heures de Notre Dame was one of the books from the library of the Duc de Berry that was left unfinished at his death. It was completed after his death and the additions pose a tantalizing problem. The book was later divided into three parts between Paris, Milan and Turin. A fire destroyed the Turin part in 1904 but the Milan part, which rather confusingly is now at Turin, contains illustrations at the foot of the pages (fig. 130) that are of extremely fine quality and may well be the work of Hubert van Eyck.

Grisaille technique, a monochrome form of painting in shades of grey or brown with white heightening, becomes important at this date. The Offices of the Blessed Virgin (Turin, Museo Civico) has illustrations of this type and the Virgin and Child (fig. 131) are shown as if seen through a window. This is probably a Flemish work, and the sculptural weight characteristic of Claus Sluter is predominant in the bulk of the draperies.

The Duc de Berry was not alone in his great patronage of illuminators. Many knights and noblemen wanted fine books for their own personal use. Among them was Jean le Meingre, Maréchal de Boucicaut. He employed an anonymous artist, known as the Maître de Boucicaut, whose chief work was a Book of Hours (Paris, Musée Jacquemart André) executed between 1410 and 1415. It must not be forgotten that we are still in the great age of chivalry and romance. The Maréchal de Boucicaut was one of the last Crusaders and Chaucer's 'verray parfit gentil knight' describes him well. This Book of Hours includes the episode of St George and the Dragon (fig. 152), a romantic subject no doubt near to the heart of such a character. The artist displays a painterly style and an inborn sense of linear perspective. Horizons are still unrealistically high, but the artist struggles for a sense of recession with twisting paths and rocks to disguise his limitations.

The Boucicaut Master seems to have worked with the Bedford Master on an illuminated manuscript of the Livre de Merveilles (Paris, Bibliothèque Nationale), which recounted the journeys of Marco Polo to the East. The Bedford Master is yet another artist whose name is unknown; he worked from *c* 1424 to 1435 for John of Lancaster, Duke of Bedford, who had been appointed Regent for the English Crown in France. Among the books he commissioned are a Breviary (Paris, Bibliothèque Nationale) and a Book of Hours (London, British Museum). The Book of Hours (fig. 151) contains a portrait of the Duchess of Bedford offering her devotion to the Madonna. St George and the Dragon again occur in the Breviary (fig. 136). These volumes are characterized by an extreme richness of decoration; many of the pages have subsidiary scenes around the main subject, and the spaces are filled with rich swags of foliage. A comparison between the Bedford and the Boucicaut paintings of St George and the Dragon is interesting. It shows that the Bedford Master has a greater sense of decoration; facial expressions have less meaning for him but his scenes are pervaded with a harmonious atmospheric light.

Yet another brother of King Charles V, the Duke of Anjou, and his duchess, Yolande of Aragon, were collectors of manuscripts. About 1414, an artist known as the Rohan Master entered the service of the Duke. Among his works is the so-called Rohan Hours (Paris, Bibliothèque Nationale). The Rohan Master had been trained in Paris and worked closely with the Master of Bedford and the Boucicaut Master. He may have come originally from Spain, the home of the Duchess Yolande, and the paintings he executed after he joined the Angevin court are certainly very different from those of his Parisian contemporaries. In the Rohan Book of Hours, Vespers opens with a painting of the Flight into Egypt (fig. 157). Here the artist has moved away from the fashionable style of the period of his association with the Paris masters, to something much more personal. He replaces the expressionless faces of the Bedford Master's figures with features which clearly show the strong emotions of the characters. He distinguishes the principal characters of the story by making them much larger than the others; in the middle distance of this scene they are shown as larger than the huntsmen in the foreground. Unlike the graceful, idealized figures of the Bedford Master, those of the Rohan Master are shorter and more robust, and far less aware of themselves. This style appealed to the Spanish duchess, and indeed, the closest comparisons to it are found in the Gothic works of Languedoc and Catalonia.

England

England's role in the International Style can be seen as early as 1377 in books written for the royal household. The Coronation Book of Richard II (London, Westminster Abbey) has close connections with the Bible written for Richard's brother-in-law, Wenzel of Bohemia. A number of late-fourteenth-century manuscripts have notes written in Low German, probably by illuminators that Richard's queen brought with her.

The great Crucifixion in the Missal written for Robert Lytlington, Abbot of Westminster (London, Westminster Abbey), can also be favourably compared with the best Bohemian manuscripts of the day, but several other styles also made an impression on the English scene.

The name of an English Dominican monk, John Siferwas, occurs in the Sherborne Missal (collection of the Duke of Northumberland) which was written between 1396 and 1407. He and Herman Scherre were the two outstanding artists of the day. There is a sketchbook in Cambridge (Fitzwilliam Museum) that is often associated with Herman Scherre, and this has birds and animals, costumes and faces, drawn with all the accurate attention to detail that Giovannino dei Grassi shows in Italy. There is absolutely no connection between the two, but this comparison merely serves to exemplify the common ideas of artists in two centres that are geographically far apart.

The Carmelite Missal (London, British Museum) is a lavishly decorated book of large proportions. It is unlikely that Herman Scherre himself decorated this book but the illustrations are close to his style and reveal striking connections with contemporary developments in Holland. Brilliant colours are used and the figures are painted with the round, doll-like faces that were so much a feature of the Dutch school.

It is typical of the international character of this movement that one of the finest Books of Hours made in England was for that same John of Lancaster, Duke of Bedford, who had commissioned the Breviary and Book of Hours from Paris. The English Bedford Hours (London, British Museum) contains a very large number of small historiated initials, some of which hold scenes from the Life of Christ. Compared with the grand illustrations of the French Bedford Master, these seem to be almost traditional and very simple, but the handling is assured and the artist shows a remarkable naturalism on a minute scale.

Italy

The impact of the International Style was so strong that it affected the early Renaissance artists of Central Italy. Even Ghiberti came momentarily under its sway. Admittedly, its origins owe much to the fourteenth-century Sienese artist, Simone Martini, but Ghiberti was working in a Florence increasingly dominated by the new spirit of the Renaissance.

It is rare to find a major Italian artist working on illuminated manuscripts, but in Florence at the end of the fourteenth century we see Lorenzo Monaco working in the monastic scriptorium of Sta Maria degli Angeli. His early manuscripts reflect the strong Florentine traditions of such artists as Orcagna, but later a refinement and an increasing delicacy come into his work through the influence of the International Style. In turn, Lorenzo Monaco's influence is seen in a work such as the Choir Book (fig. 126) in the library of San Marco at Florence. Even at his most Gothic, Lorenzo still has a narrative strength and a grandeur to which northern artists could only aspire. Yet the lines of his drapery are soft and fluid, the figures tall and elegant, and he imparts that sense of introspective mysticism that is so much a part of the International Style.

This new movement found greatest favour in the more northerly cities of Verona and Milan. North Italian artists had established themselves in Paris and in Prague, where, of course, they assimilated the new style. Equally, the artists who remained in Italy came under its influence. Giovannino dei Grassi, born *c* 1370, is the supreme Italian exponent of the International Style. A sketchbook at Bergamo shows his passionate interest in the actual observation of birds and animals, balanced by his courtly delight in costumes and fabrics. He is thought to be the artist of a Breviary known as Il Beroldo (Milan, Biblioteca Trivulziana). Much of his fresh observation is lost in this work, painted to commission and limited by the set illustrations (fig. 118), but his vitality shines through and is well shown in the small scene of David and Goliath. The page from the copy of Dante's *Divine Comedy* (Milan, Biblioteca Trivulziana) shown in fig. 123 contains drawings of lesser quality than those of Grassi, but again the courtly aspect of Milanese art is underlined.

The *Taccuinum Sanitas* was a 'book of reason' with a short text and a great number of illustrations which, like the *Biadaiolo* in Florence, are of humble subjects painted with careful attention to detail. Among the copies of this work written in Lombardy is the book now in Paris (Bibliothèque Nationale). This includes scenes of butter merchants selling their goods (fig. 116) and of tailors at work (fig. 117). One imagines that it was just this sort of illustration that impressed the artists working in Paris at this time, for the realism of intimate detail is powerful and all-important.

The ruling dynasty of Milan, the Visconti, had close political associations with the Burgundian dukes. The Visconti's principal artistic achievement was the building of Milan Cathedral under their patronage. They did not neglect manuscripts, and among the artists working for them was Michelino da Besozzo. This artist was responsible for the frontispiece to the Funeral Oration composed in honour of Gian Galeazzo Visconti (Paris, Bibliothèque Nationale). Idealized form and ethereal grace are combined, in the scene of the Christ Child bestowing reward on Gian Galeazzo, to such perfection that Michelino can well be compared with the best French and Flemish artists of the period. The Winter Missal of the Visconti (Milan, Biblioteca Ambrosiana) was illuminated for them by a certain Anovelo da Imbonate. In comparison with the finest works of Lombardy, this Missal (fig. 119) is rather monotonously illustrated, and the artist's national stature is hardly detectable in the abundance of decorative courtly detail.

For a long time Venice remained in close contact with Byzantium, and it was not until the end of the thirteenth century that an independent style emerged. Few religious books of this period have survived, and we must trace the stylistic developments in Mariegole – books commemorating the foundations of guilds – and other secular works. Still strongly under the influence of Byzantine examples, the artists drew their inspiration from a variety of sources and combined them into a rather unsatisfactory style of their own. Towards the end of the fourteenth century a new wave of influence from the North can be detected and it was this that revitalized their art. If we were faced with the page from the Invasion of Spain (Venice, Biblioteca Marciana) (fig. 127) and shown it in isolation, it would be far easier to suggest a date than to localize its origin. The international character of Venetian illumination at this date is paramount and bears witness to the movement's importance.

Bohemia

During the first half of the fourteenth century, the artistic centres of Bohemia had been amply prepared for the great flowering of manuscript illumination after 1350. The important implications of the foundation of the University of Prague have already been mentioned. At this moment, Bohemia came to the forefront of artistic development, and remained there for half a century.

A good example of the transition towards the new style can be seen in the illustrations from the History of the New Testament (Munich, Staatsbibliothek) (fig. 108). This shows Christ and Mary Magdalene in a garden enclosed by a wicket fence. This is an early example of a subject that became very popular during the fifteenth century in Germany. The figures are firmly placed on the ground, and behind the fence we see the small clumps of trees that remind us of the art of Jean Pucelle.

The chancellor of Charles IV was called Jean de Streda, or John of Neumarkt. He may have been responsible for Petrarch's visit to Prague and the two certainly carried on a correspondence. The Liber Viaticus of Jean de Streda was a breviary especially written to be taken on journeys, and it is now preserved in the National Library at Prague. It was written *c* 1360 and contains historiated initials in a style clearly based on Italian prototypes. The figures are firmly constructed and well arranged in space, and in the borders the acanthus foliage of the Bolognese school is introduced. Closely connected with *Liber Viaticus* is the *Laus Mariae* of Conrad von Hainburg (Prague, National Library). The Presentation in the Temple (fig. 112) again shows this ambitious attempt at the construction of space. The soft swinging curves of the drapery do not hide the forms beneath, and the overall impression is one of rounded softness.

The group of books written for Jean de Streda is followed by a collection of manuscripts written for the successor of Charles IV, King Wenzel of Bohemia. The principal works of this group are the two bibles written in German and a number of secular manuscripts including the poems of Wolfram and an astrological treatise in Munich. The illustrations of the last book include skilfully drawn birds and animals and can be favourably compared with the sketchbook of Giovannino dei Grassi at Bergamo. In general, the books of King Wenzel are much more lavishly illustrated than those of Jean de Streda, and there is some modification of the Italian influence.

By about 1400 the style that reached such perfection in Prague seems to fade away. It is replaced by a far more sketchy style of illumination, and books are decorated with brisk line-drawings in pen and ink. Part of the reason for the abrupt change in style may be due to the increasing use of paper instead of parchment, and its subsequent limitations. The heritage of the soft delicate style of the Prague illuminators was taken over by artists who worked on a larger scale, panel-painters such as Master Theodorik, who worked for the Bohemian royal house at the Castle of Karlstein. Illustrations in the Lüneburg Sachsenspiegel (Lüneburg, Ratsbibliothek) *c* 1400 retain the rich painterly quality of the Bohemian school, but this is probably the work of an artist who painted the 'Golden Altarpiece', and was renowned as a panel-painter. Similarly, a page of the Crucifixion from a manuscript now in Basle (private collection) can be most closely compared with panels by the so-called Veronica Master.

As the fifteenth century progressed in Germany, the style originated in those Prague manuscripts became more emphatically fluid and its immediate freshness was lost. Faces were painted with almost cloying sweetness, and the term 'soft style' is justifiable in more than one sense.

The International Style did not come abruptly to a close, but in each country national characteristics again began to reassert themselves. In Germany, we see this change as early as 1405, whereas in France the style was perpetuated by the Bedford Master and the Boucicaut Master for another twenty years.

As in earlier centuries, it was Northern Europe that saw the important advances in manuscript illumination, and the last section of this introduction will be dealing almost exclusively with the manuscripts of France and Flanders. Of course, the other countries continued to produce fine books; for example, Mantegna is known to have been a fine illuminator. But again, book illustration in Italy followed the advances made in more monumental works of art.

René d'Anjou

Before we turn to the main streams of development in France and Flanders during the fifteenth century, some mention must be made of René d'Anjou (1409–1480). René was Duke of Anjou, Count of Provence, and King of Naples and Sicily although he lost the latter to the Aragonese in 1443. He was thus a man whose interests constantly gravitated towards the south. His courts at Anjou and at Aix were cosmopolitan centres where he surrounded himself with Italian scholars and Flemish illuminators. René d'Anjou, a deeply religious man, was also an intellectual who wrote fine poetry.

A number of illuminated manuscripts by one man are closely connected with René's own writings, and so it is often thought that René was also an artist. This is a keenly debated question to which a definite answer will probably never be found, but the paintings have a spiritual quality and an originality not found in the work of his immediate contemporaries. The romance of *Cuer des Amours Epris* (Vienna, Nationalbibliothek) was composed by René in 1457. It is an allegorical romance and in fig. 154 we see the lovelorn Cuer sleeping while his companion reads the magic inscription on the well-head. A translucency pervades these paintings, and the artist boldly shows night scenes; in this illustration the sun is seen rising over the meadows. The early morning light floods across the fields, casting deep shadows behind the figures. René also wrote the *Mortifiement de la Vaine Plaisance* (Brussels, Bibliothèque Royale) after the death of his first wife. It is a Christian allegory on the futility of earthly life and the illustrations (fig. 156) reflect the deeply spiritual content of the text. The same hand appears in the illustrations of Boccaccio's *Teseide* (Vienna, Nationalbibliothek) (fig. 155) where we see an artist who could illustrate lively, bustling narratives. Cherishing the old chivalrous ideals of the fourteenth century, René d'Anjou founded the Order of the Knights of St Maurice, and his interest in courtly traditions can be seen in his Book of Tournaments (Paris, bibliothèque Nationale) written between 1460 and 1465. In fig. 153, we see noblemen selecting their weapons, and here the artist reveals himself as a skilful decorator, relishing every detail of the ceremony.

René, in common with the earlier artist, the Master of the Rohan Hours, had neither school nor followers. An isolated and enchanting artist, René would attract our attention even if this were his only accomplishment, but the sum of his talents, his nobility of mind and deed, make him a truly remarkable person.

Fifteenth-Century Flemish Illumination

The rising importance of Flanders itself as a centre for manuscript illumination can, to a great extent, be explained by the continued patronage of the Dukes of Burgundy. After the death of Philip the Bold, Philip the Good later inherited the domains of Burgundy and Flanders. Unlike his ancestor, Philip the Good chose to live in the northerly area of his kingdom, and had residences in Ghent and in Brussels, at Lille and The Hague. The Flemish artists who had earlier flocked south to the court at Dijon were now able to work on their home ground. Following in the family tradition, Philip was a great collector of illuminated books. Historians such as David Aubert and Jean Mansel were also at his court. He occasionally gave work to Parisian artists, but generally the Duke found abundant talent nearer at hand.

Among the finest illustrators working for the Duke was Jean Tavernier, whose style can be seen in David Aubert's *Conquests of Charlemagne* (Brussels, Bibliothèque Royale) (fig. 147). Tavernier, working during the mid-fifteenth century, had an unrivalled mastery of the grisaille technique and in monochrome shades was able to give a vivid account of daily life. In contrast, Loyset Liedet reveals a rather stiff, dry style in his illuminations of the *Histoires Romaines* (Paris, Bibliothèque de l'Arsenal) (fig. 140). He did have a good sense of composition and was a very prolific artist, but his work compares unfavourably with that of Tavernier.

Simon Marmion, who was known in his day as the 'prince of illuminators', was a Frenchman who also worked for Philip the Good. He illustrated the *Fleur des Histoires* (Brussels, Bibliothèque Royale) (fig. 139) and his hand has also been attributed to the frontispiece (fig. 138) of the

Chroniques de Hainaut (Brussels, Bibliothèque Royale) of 1448. The influence of Roger van der Weyden and of van Eyck is keenly felt in the fine composition and the clear understanding of space. The size of the hall, allowing plenty of room for all the onlookers, is carefully indicated by the tiled floor that leads the eye back into depth. Each face is individually treated and among the onlookers one can single out Chancellor Rolin who appears again in the painting of the Madonna by Jan van Eyck (Paris, Louvre).

Philip the Good was succeeded by his son Charles the Bold in 1467, who also employed great numbers of illuminators, but in 1477 Charles the Bold was killed in battle against the King of France. The established workshops in Ghent and Bruges continued to produce books of extremely high quality, but the artists who influenced them now were not those great pioneers, Roger van der Weyden and van Eyck, but Hugo van der Goes and Gerard David. One of the triumphs of this later Flemish school of illumination is the Grimani Breviary (Venice, Biblioteca Marciana). Several artists had a hand in the many illustrations (figs. 158 and 159), which are of the highest quality. Space and lighting no longer present any serious problems to the artists, but it must not be forgotten that this was written at the beginning of the sixteenth century.

Two great families stand out in this last great school of manuscript illumination: the Bening family and the Horebout dynasty. Sanders Bening had three active children who worked for him, and Gerhard Horebout was the father of perhaps the first woman illuminator, Susanna, who later moved to England and married a member of Henry VIII's court. The *Hortulus Animae* of Margaret of Austria (Vienna, Nationalbibliothek) (figs. 172 and 173), which probably came from the workshop of Horebout, has charming illustrations set in a wide border of decoration. These borders are far removed from the foliate decorations of earlier centuries and show the first signs of the Northern delight in still-life painting. Flowers and fruit are treated with minute perfection, and the pansies and arbutus blossoms are skilfully modelled with light so that they seem to spring from the surface of the page. The borders of these pages are certainly the most rewarding part of these later books, for the treatment of the main subjects is good but in no way inspiring.

Jean Fouquet and Later French Illumination

After 1420, the importance of Paris declined, owing to the English occupation, the madness of the king, and the terrible political strife. The metropolis no longer attracted artists, and we see the rise of provincial schools of painting.

Jean Fouquet, who was born *c* 1420 at Tours, was the finest French painter of the day. He must have been highly thought of by his contemporaries, for we know that he went to Rome and painted a portrait of the Pope, Eugenius IV. Unfortunately, no record survives of Fouquet's painting before his trip (1445–1447), but his journey to Italy left a permanent mark on his work. His name occurs in only one manuscript, the *Antiquités Judaïques*, but others are easily attributable to him on stylistic grounds.

The Hours of Etienne Chevalier (Chantilly, Musée Condé) are the finest testimony to Fouquet's greatness. Etienne Chevalier was Minister of Finance to the King and on almost every page his name is prominently displayed. A lifelike portrait of Chevalier and his patron saint is shown in the Adoration of the Virgin (fig. 162). This book was probably made soon after the artist's return from Italy, and it shows the closest connections with the paintings he saw there. The setting of this scene shows a mixture of Classical and Gothic architecture, of Northern and Southern ideals of beauty. Reflections of the art of Fra Angelico can be seen in the half-turned figures and the grouping of the angels, but the Madonna is much closer to the style of the Early Netherlandish artists. Her blue robe, heightened with gold, spreads over the floor in rich undulating folds that remind us of the Master of Flémalle. Although deeply impressed with the art of Italy, Fouquet remains an essentially Northern artist.

Soon after the completion of the Book of Hours for Etienne Chevalier, Fouquet received a commission from the King, Charles VII, to illustrate the *Grandes Chroniques de France* (Paris, Bibliothèque Nationale). This was no easy task, but Fouquet had the power to bring the rather unexciting historical events to life. He shows (figs. 165 and 168) a dignified approach to the subject and enhances his scenes with careful detail.

The *Antiquités Judaïques* (Paris, Bibliothèque Nationale) was yet another of the books left unfinished by that great connoisseur, Jean, duc de Berry. Fouquet was asked to complete the illustrations started by the Limbourg brothers. The scenes are crowded with figures and seem to vibrate with activity. Fouquet did not feel it necessary to put his scenes in historical settings, and Jericho (fig. 164) is shown as a small French village with a river meandering around the hillside in the distance.

In 1469, the King founded the Order of St Michael, and he must have commissioned Fouquet to illustrate the frontispiece to the Book of Statutes (Paris, Bibliothèque Nationale). This page (fig. 170) reaffirms Fouquet's skill as a portrait painter, for a number of the knights can be singled out as important members of the court circle.

Jean Fouquet no doubt had a large following of admirers and pupils. Among his most eminent followers was Jean Bourdichon. It was Bourdichon who carried the tradition of manuscript illumination on into the sixteenth century; in comparison with the great master his art must be considered less important. He made Fouquet his example but could never match the latter's fresh eloquence. From *c* 1484, Bourdichon was court painter to King Charles VII, and among his works is the Book of Hours written for the Queen, Anne of Brittany (Paris, Bibliothèque Nationale). The illustrations to this book (fig. 176) comprise large, heavy paintings of solid figures set in an architectural framework. They are competent but rather cold and mechanical. The work of Jean Bourdichon can also be detected in the scene of the Centaur killed by Lapiths (fig. 171) from the Hours of Charles d'Angoulême (Paris, Bibliothèque Nationale). Tremendous excitement should fill this dramatic scene, but one feels that Fouquet would have imparted this feeling with far more effect. Bourdichon worked for a man who tried to perpetuate the chivalrous ideals of earlier times, and bearing in mind that Bourdichon did not die until 1521, it is obvious that he was a consciously retrogressive artist, totally unmoved by the great movements of the Renaissance in Italy and Flanders.

At this time, the art of illuminating manuscripts, which had flourished through many centuries, came abruptly to a close. The Renaissance was to affect every facet of man's intellectual and artistic existence. The conception of painting underwent a fundamental change, assuming forms which were to continue into modern times. Portraiture and landscape-painting, large-scale religious paintings on canvas and panel were the new order. At the same time, the invention of printing burst upon the tranquil world of illuminated, handwritten books like some undreamed-of automation in our modern world. As the printing of books gathered momentum, they changed from being the privilege of the wealthy few to the joy of great numbers of mankind. Even if such technical advances had not been achieved at this period, the change of attitude to religion, the questionings of the great Renaissance intellectuals, the attacks of the Reformation, and the ultimate rise of materialism would have sufficed to undermine the simple piety which, in a relatively static world, had produced this lasting example of personal endeavour, the illuminated manuscript.

Medieval Manuscript Painting

Illustrations

AESTAS
GLORIA DIEI
FLORIDUS
FRUGIFER
TERCENTENIS
BIS Q: TRICENIS
QUINQ: DIEBUS
ANNUS
AUTUMNUS FERTILIS
HIEMPS HORRIBILIS
NOX
IANUARIUS · FEBRUARIUS · MARCIUS ·
APRILIS · MAIUS
IUNIUS ·
IULIUS ·
AUGUSTUS · SEPTIMBER · OCTIMBER · NOUIMBER · DECIMBER

1

4

5

6

7

8

9

TV MANDASTI MANDATA TVA CUSTODIRE NIMIS.

11

13

15

EGO SV̄ HOSTIV̄ PER ME SI QVIS INTRO IERIT SALVABITVR ET PASCVA INVENIET.
ITE IN ORBEM VNIVERSVM PREDICATE EVVANGELIVM MEV̄ OMNI CREATURAE.

17

HILDEFVNS

INNOMINE DNI INCIPIT
OPUSCULUM PTATIO
NIS INQUA EXPRIMIT
HUMILIS DEVOTIO
ATQ; PIA CONFESSIO
SEQUITUR
S
LUMEN VERU

21

NE DVBITET QVISQVĀ DE MORTE RESVMERE VITAM.
TAMQVAM NON POSSET HOMO QVOD DOMINVS POTVISSET.
NOLVERAT SOLVS DE MORTE RESVRGERE XPICTVS.
SED SECVM PLVRES DEDIT ECCE RESVRGERE TESTIS.

IACOB
EGO IN ALTISSIMIS HABITO
VIDEO DNM FACIE AD FACIEM
HIC·SVNT·TRANQVILLE·SEDES·EX·GAVDIA·MILLE·

23

DAS ABIUD
PER·TE·SEN
HABENDUS
MEUS ISTE
TIRE·PATER
AZOR ADIU
NOMEN A
DEO PATRE
CECLAMAT
ELEAZAR
PE CORONANS
SIC ELIUD
TOR MEUS
NOMINE SUP
PLANTANS
DICITUR ANGLS
EST SPECIE
TYPICUS
IOSEPH QUI

25

27

29

31

33

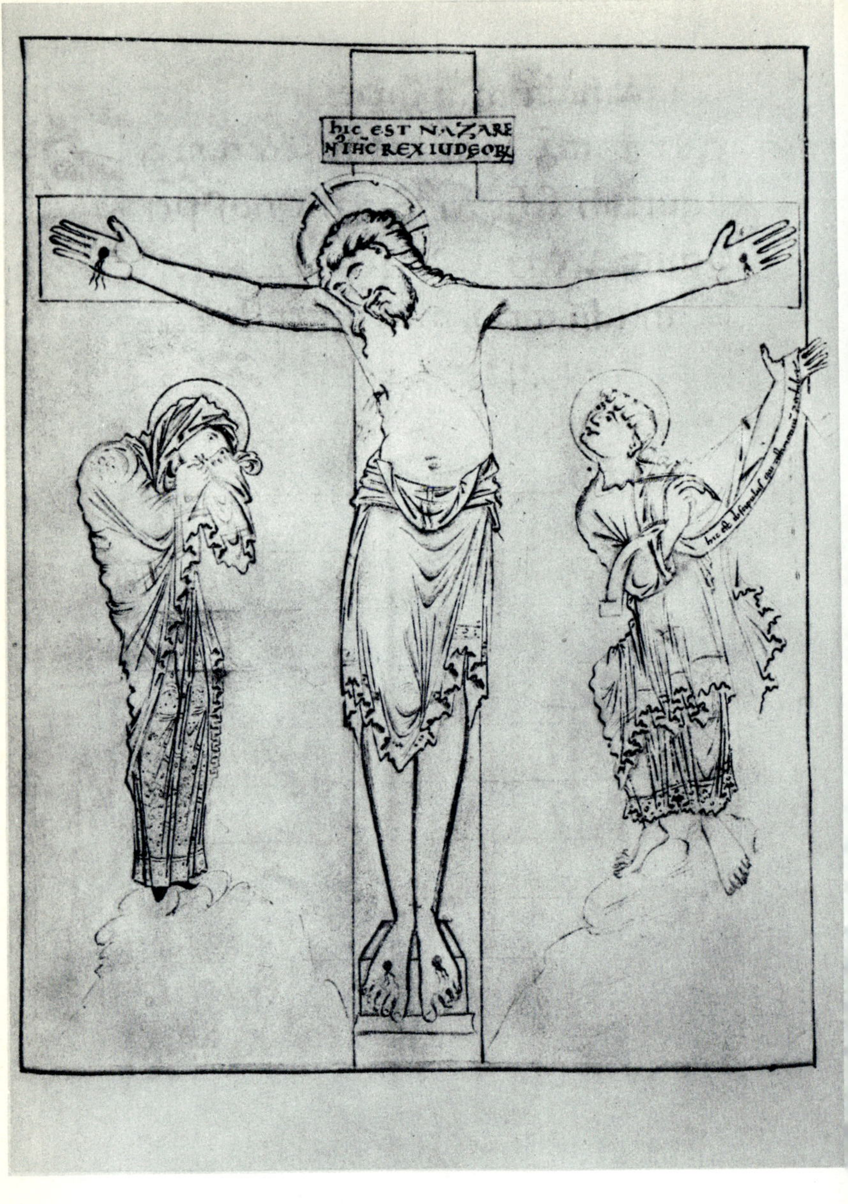
hic est nazare
n ihc rex iudeor

On þam þriddan dæge hi man lædde to þam cwearterne · 7 he cwæþ ta
naþ 7 swa ic eow bebead þæt ge magon libban · ic ondræde me god · gyf ic siht
nabbe · beo eower an broðor her on cwearterne · 7 fare ge mid þam hwæte
þe ge bohton to eowrum husum · 7 lædaþ eowerne geongestan broþor to me ·
hi didon swa he him bebead · 7 cwædon him betwynan · be ge wyrhtum we
þoliaþ þas þing · we syngodon on urum breþer · 7 we gesawon hys angsu
nysse · þa he us georne friþes bæd · 7 we him nanes ne tiþodon · forþam
com þis geswinc ofer us · Ða cwæþ ruben cweþe ge · ne sæde ic eow ne
singie ge on þam cnapan · 7 ge me ne gehyrdon · Nu hine man wrihþ ·
hy nyston þæt iosep hyge cneow · 7 he wende hine ut hwon fram him 7 weop ·
7 wende eft to him · 7 nam simeon · 7 band hine beforan him · 7 bead his þegnum
þæt hi gefyldon heora saccas mid hwæte · 7 ledon dearninga heora ælces
feoh on hys sacc · 7 forme te to etan · 7 hi didon swa ·

7 hi foron 7 læddon heora hwæte on heora assan · Ða hi be wege wæron · þa
undide heora an hys sacc · 7 wolde sillan hys assan fodor · þa cwæþ he to his
gebroþrum · þa he þæt feoh geseah on þæs saccas muþe · Her ic hæbbe
funden min feoh on þis saccas muþe · Ða wurdon hi afyrhte · 7 cwæ
don him betweonan · hwæt is þis þæt god us dide ·

BRITISH MUSEUM

37

Unicornis qui et rinoceros a grecis dicitur. hanc habet
naturam. pusillum animal est simile hedo. acerrimum
nimis. unum cornu habens in medio capite et nullus venator
eum capere potest. Sed hoc argumento capitur. Puella virgo
ducitur ubi moratur et ibi dimittitur in silva sola. At ille mox
ut viderit eam in silvis in sinu eius et complectitur eam et sic com-
prehenditur. Sic et dominus noster ihesus christus est spiritualiter unicornis de
quo dicitur. Et dilectus quemadmodum filius unicornium. Et in
psalmo alio. Exaltabitur sicut unicornis cornu meum.
Et zacharias. Suscitavit nobis cornu salutis in domo da

3

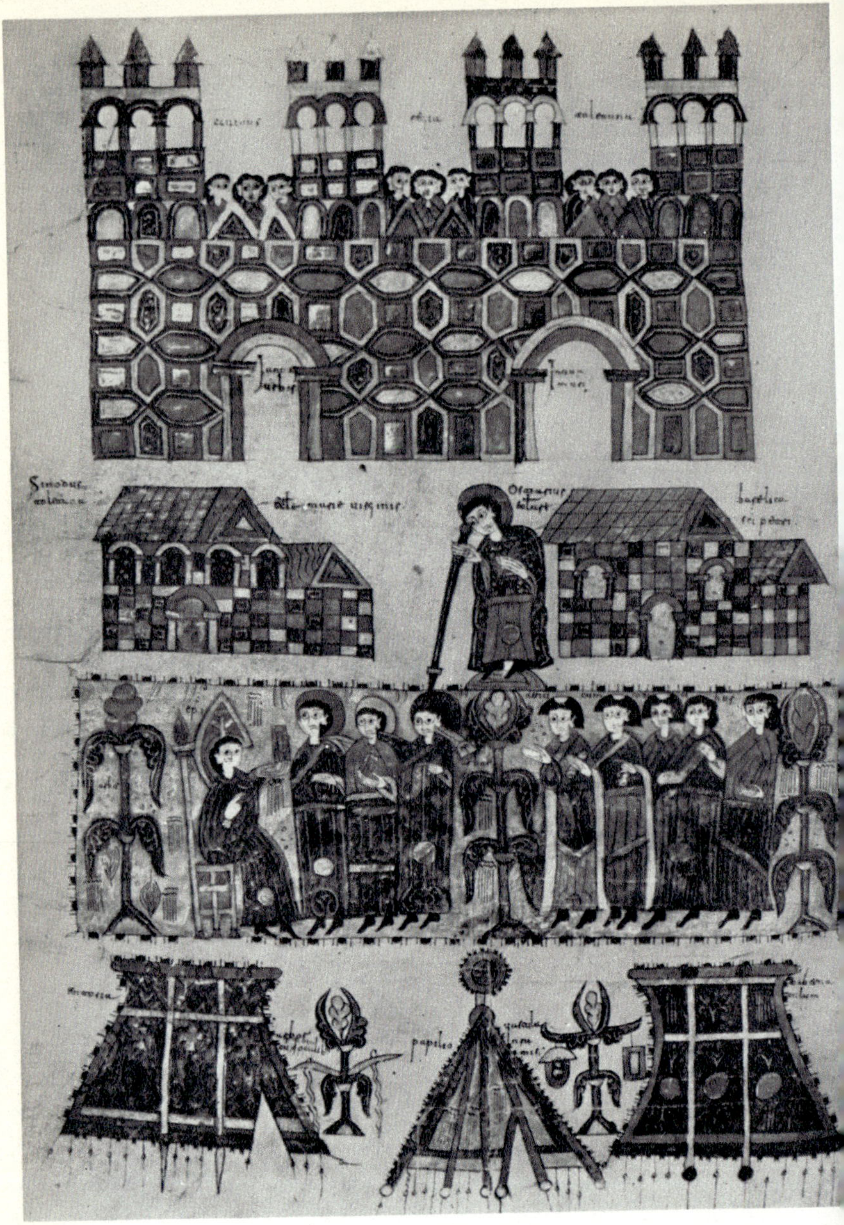

45

Columba
Archa noe

INCIPIT LIBER PRI
MUS MACHABEORŪ

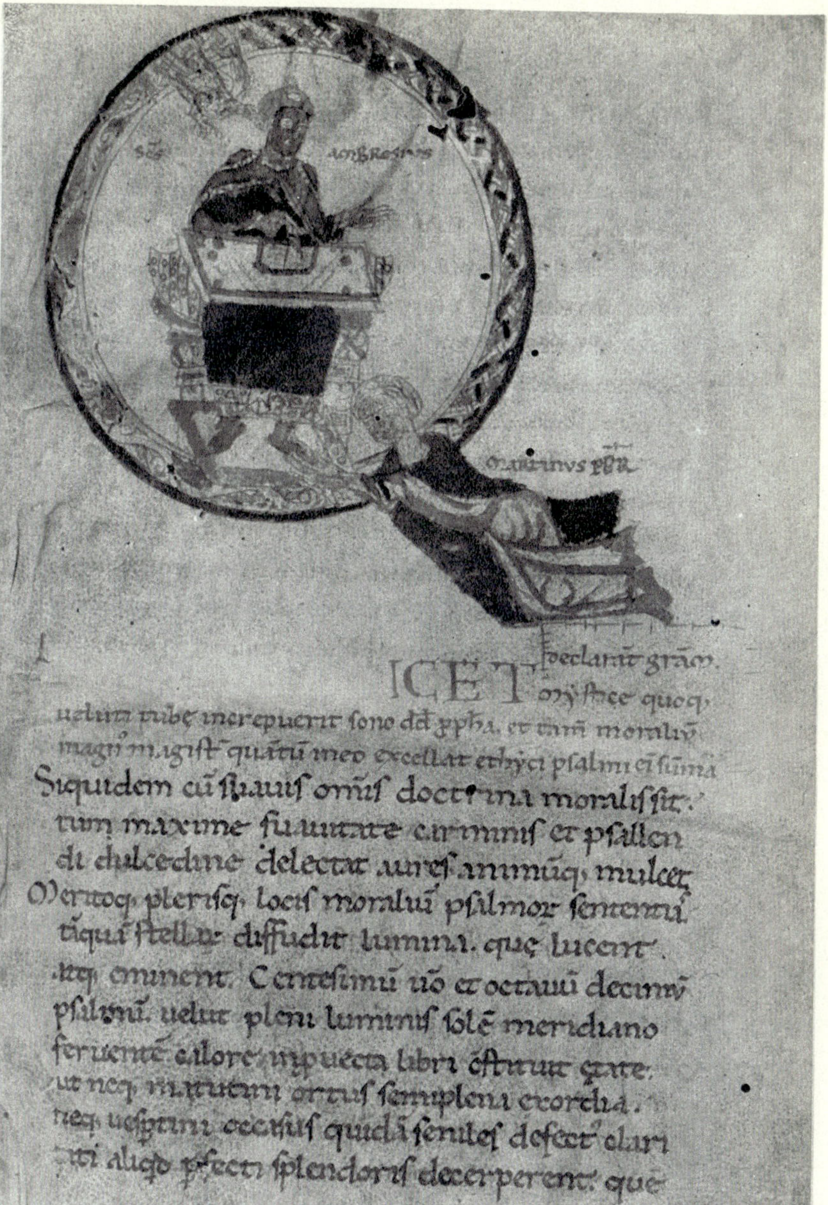
Scs Augustinus
Martinus pbr

ICET ... declarauit gram...
... omis haec quoq;
uelut tube increpuerit sono dei ppha. et tam moralis
magis magist quantu meo excellat ethyci psalmi ei summa
Siquidem cu sit suauis omnis doctrina moralis sit.
tum maxime suauitate carminis et psallen
di dulcedine delectat aures animuq; mulcet.
Meritoq; plerisq; locis moraliu psalmor sententias
tamqua stellar diffudit lumina. que lucent
atq; eminent. Centesimu uo et octauu decimu
psalmu. uelut pleni luminis sole meridiano
feruente calore in pfecta libri cstituit etate.
ut neq; matutini ortus semiplena exordia.
neq; uespertini occasus quida seniles defect clari
tati aliqd pfecti splendoris decerperent. que

EX PLI CI VNT CA PI TV LA

51

VE RE
QVIA DIGNV
ETIVS TV EST
AEQVV ETSALVTAR

53

NITI
VM
SCI
BER
GENERA
TIONIS

rex medorum:' subiugauerat multas

59

61

culo sum scribam aliquid gratum uob·
utile ecclesie dignum posteris; presentium quippe
iudiciis non satis moueor· qui in utramque;
partem aut amore labuntur aut odio;

EXPLICIT PROLOGUS·

INCIPIT DANIEL PROPHETA·

Offense vestre dominus vindex valet esse

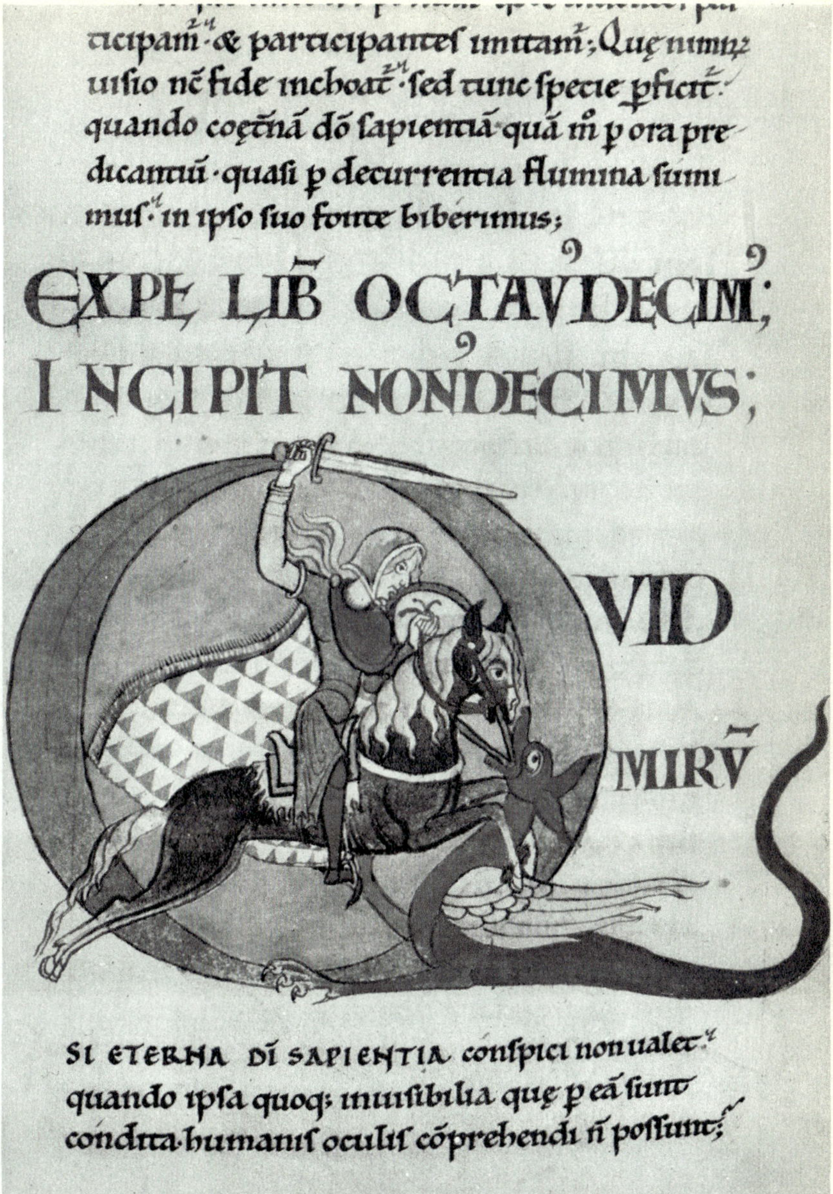
ticipam̄ · & participantes imitam̄; Quę nimirum
uisio nē fide inchoat · sed tunc specie pficit ·
quando coętnā dō sapientiā · quā nī p ora pre
dicantiū · quasi p decurrentia flumina sumi
mus · in ipso suo fonte biberimus;

EXPL LIB̄ OCTAVDECIM;

INCIPIT NONDECIMVS;

QVID MIRV̄ SI ETERNA DI SAPIENTIA conspici non ualet ·
quando ipsa quoq; inuisibilia quę p eā sunt
condita · humanis oculis cōprehendi n̄ possunt;

cit uię uiř; Aduentū
ex parte retulerat: q
condidit: alia qua rede
one narrauit: extremi
s ait; Ecce hec ex parte
parua stillam sermonis
ū. quid terribile in hac
ione cognosceum: exim
ū. uelut tenuis ad nos
nat; Et qs poterit to
s intueri. Ac si apte di
uranda uix ferim. sono
ei aduentū. q̄ uirtute
i aduentus illi. etiā dauid
: Ds manifestus ueniet.
is in conspectu ei ardebit
s ualida; Hunc sophonia
; Iuxta ē dies dñi magni.
diei dñi amara. tribu
ies illa. dies tribulatio
mitatis & miserię. die
es nebulę & turbinis.
rrorē & districti exa
i. beatus iob tonitruū
; considerans ait: contur
ę. qr uenit dies dñi; q
aliginis: dies nubis &
dñi. & tribulis ualde;
ā incōprehensibili sit
agnitudo qua in sedā
ne utrūq; ppendimus.

EXPL LIB SEPTIM DECIM;
INCIPIT LIB XVIII;

PLERUQ:
in sacro eloquio sic nonnulla mystica descri
buntur. ut tamē iuxta narratione hystoricā
plata uideantr; Sed sepe dicta talia in eadē
hystorica narratione pmixta sunt. pque
suppicies hystorię cuncta cassetr; Quę dū ni
chil hystoricū resonant. aliud mens inquirere
lectorē cogunt; His enī dictis quę apta credi
mus. eū iniecta aliq obscuri inuenim. quasi
quibdā stimulis pungim. ut ad aliqua alti
intelligenda uigilem. & obscuri plata sen
tiam. ea etiā quę apte dicta putauim; Cūq
beatus iob de sermone dñi & magnitudine to
nitrui loqueretr. eisdē uerbis pti subinfert;

REVE
RENTIS
SIMO
ETSCTISSIMO
FRI LEANDRO
COEPO:
GREGORI
SERVVS
SERVORV DI;

uoniam quidem multi conati sunt or
dinare narrationem que in nobis com
plete sunt rerum. sicut tradiderunt no
bis qui ab initio ipsi uiderunt et mi
nistri fuerunt sermonis. uisum est et
michi assecuto a principio omnib; di
ligenter ex ordine tibi scribere optime

et maiestas dñi impleuit illud;
pharao
filia pharaonis
INCIPIT
LIBER.
EX
O
DUS:
E
SUNT
NOMI
NA
FILIORU ISRAHEL:

69

SAVVALO · MONACVS
AM

IU DA S
tabnaculum foederis dni
P OSTMORTEM
IOSUE CONSU
LUERUNT FILII

73

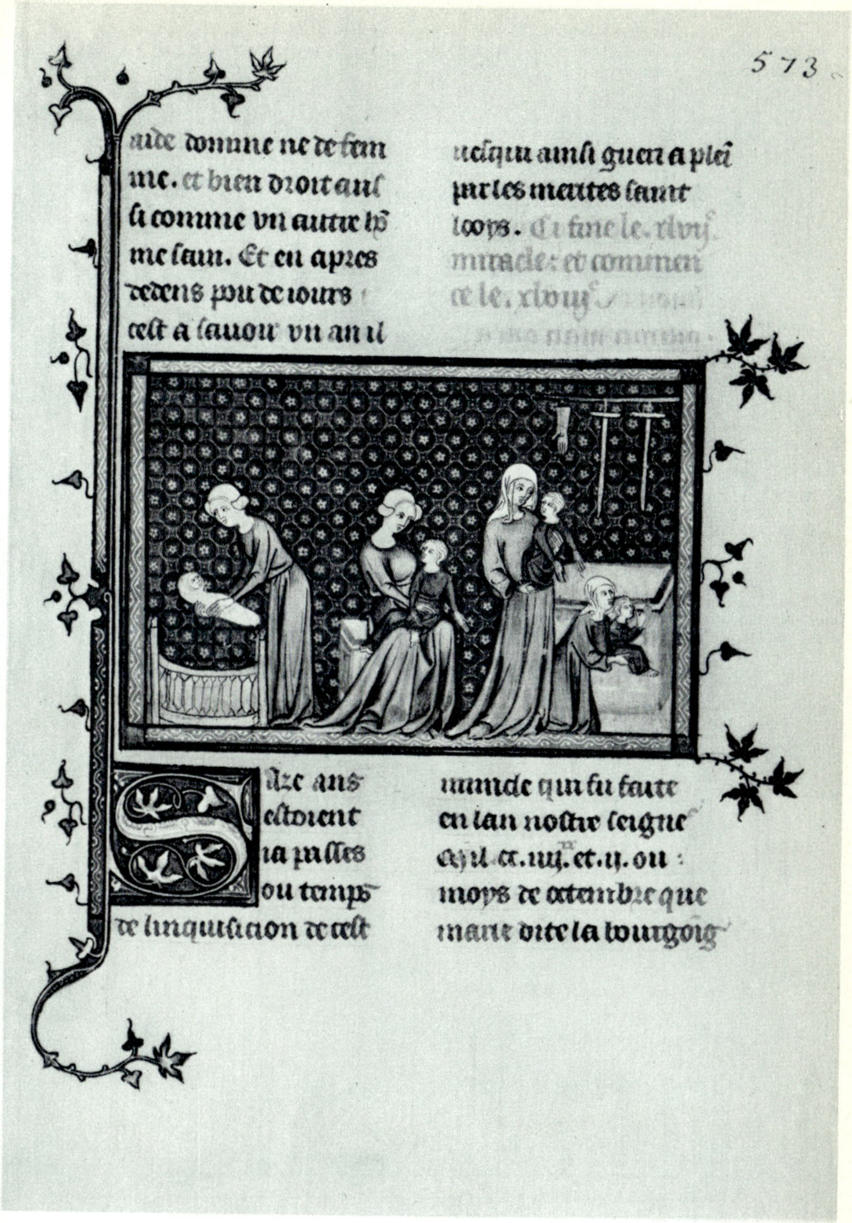
573

uide homme ne de fem
me. et bien droit auf
si comme un autre hō
me sain. Et en apres
dedens pou de iours
cest a sauoir un an il
uesquit ainsi gueri a plei
par les merites saint
loys. Ci fine le .xlvij.
miracle: et commen
ce le .xlviij.e

Seize ans
sestoient
ia passes
ou temps
de linquisition de cest
miracle qui fu faite
en lan nostre seigne
ur .m.cc.iiij.xx.et.ij. ou
moys de octembre que
marie dite la bourgoig

iohannes
euangelista
vidi ⁊ aliud mirabile
signum in celū de mulie
re ⁊ eius filio ⁊ de draco
ne rufo ⁊ de templo ⁊ ar
cha testamenti in eo.
Mulier amicta sole
habens coronam
stellarum duodecim
que peperit filium
masculum ⁊ draco
archangelus michael pug
nat cū dracone
bolo ⁊ angeli eius cū
eo.
Nunc facta est salus et
⁊ potestas xpi eius.

79

Photo B.N.

81

Si come diex fu amenez devant pilate.

IV VI

Cy commence le sixte livre ou quel il determine de la division des especes de democracie et de olygarchie · et met les princeys ou offices des policies · et c'est aussi come perfection et acomplissement du quart livre · et contient · xiij chap

Ou premier chap il propose son entencion.

Ou secont chapitre il met les supposicions et condicions et proprietez de democracie.

Ou tiers chapitre il traicte d'une question du droit democratique.

Ou quart il determine de quelles genz et de quelle maniere est la meilleur espece de democracie.

Ou quint ... mocracie.

Ou ... il monstre par quelles lois

Cy commence vng prologue sur le
commencement de la bible comment
[L]a sainte escripture se
puet raisonnablement
par quatre manieres
exposer · premierement
selonc la lettre et selonc
listoire Secondement
selonc lallegorie cestadire selonc la foy
et selonc les choses que nous devons
croire · La tierce maniere selonc la ana
gogie cestadire en appliquant la sainte
escripture aux biens de paradis les
quelz nous attendons et lesquelz
devons esperance avoir · le iiii sens
cest selonc la tropologie Cestadire q
la sainte escripture est appliquee a

par quatre sens ou par quatre manieres
se puet la sainte escripture exposer
bonnes meurs et a linstruction de
bonne vie et selonc charite Et pource
ou proces de cest livre quant lexposi
tion sera selonc listoire il sera notte
et figure et pareillement des autres
expositions [E]t a ce propos Saint
gregoire ou prologue de ses moralitez
dit que la sainte escripture si est comme
une riviere et vrayement bien mer
veilleuse car tout ensemble et en vng
temps est petite et basse haulte et parfonde
et en tant dit il est par telle maniere
que vng aignel y puet aler a pie et
vng elephant y puet noer [C]ar
laignel qui de toutes bestelettes est

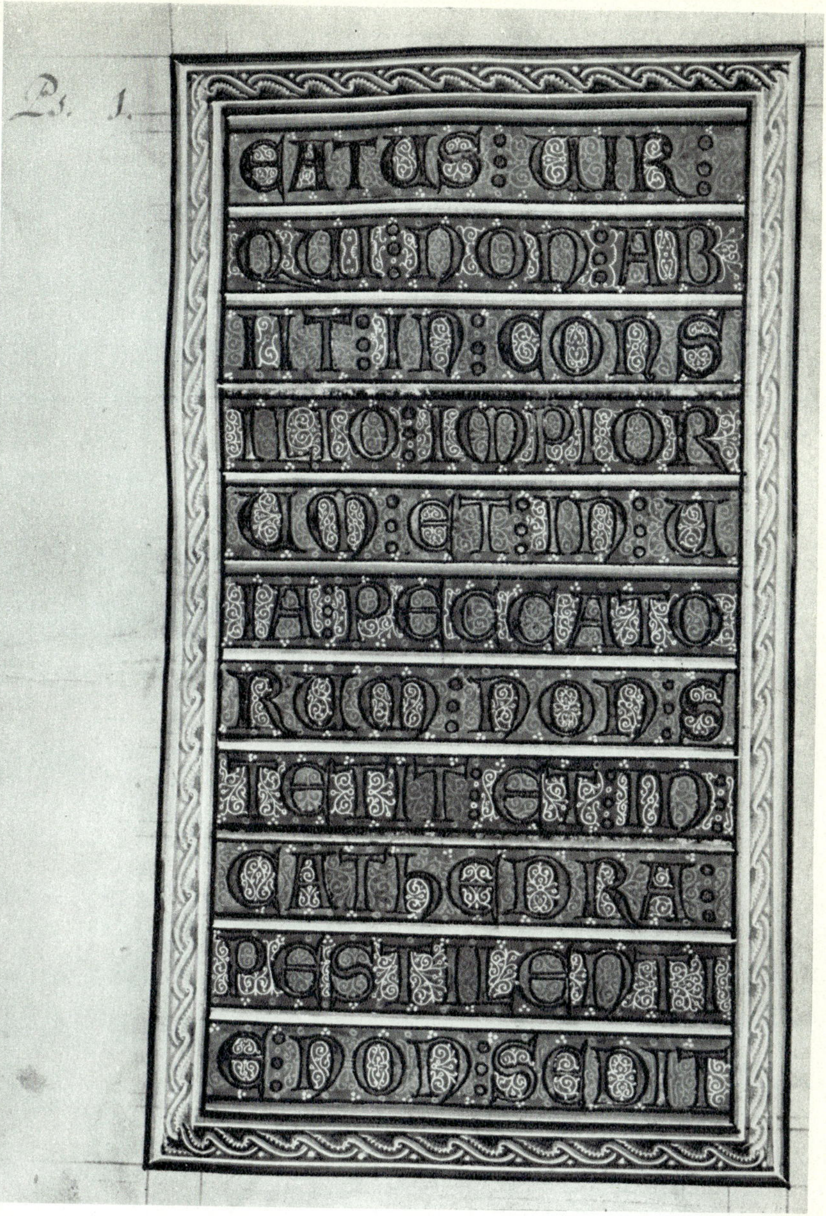
Ps. 1.
EATUS : UIR :
QUI : NON : AB
IIT : IN : CONS
ILIO : IMPIOR
UM : ET : IN : U
IA : PECCATO
RUM : NON : S
TETIT : ET : IN :
CATHEDRA :
PESTILENTI
E : NON : SEDIT

91

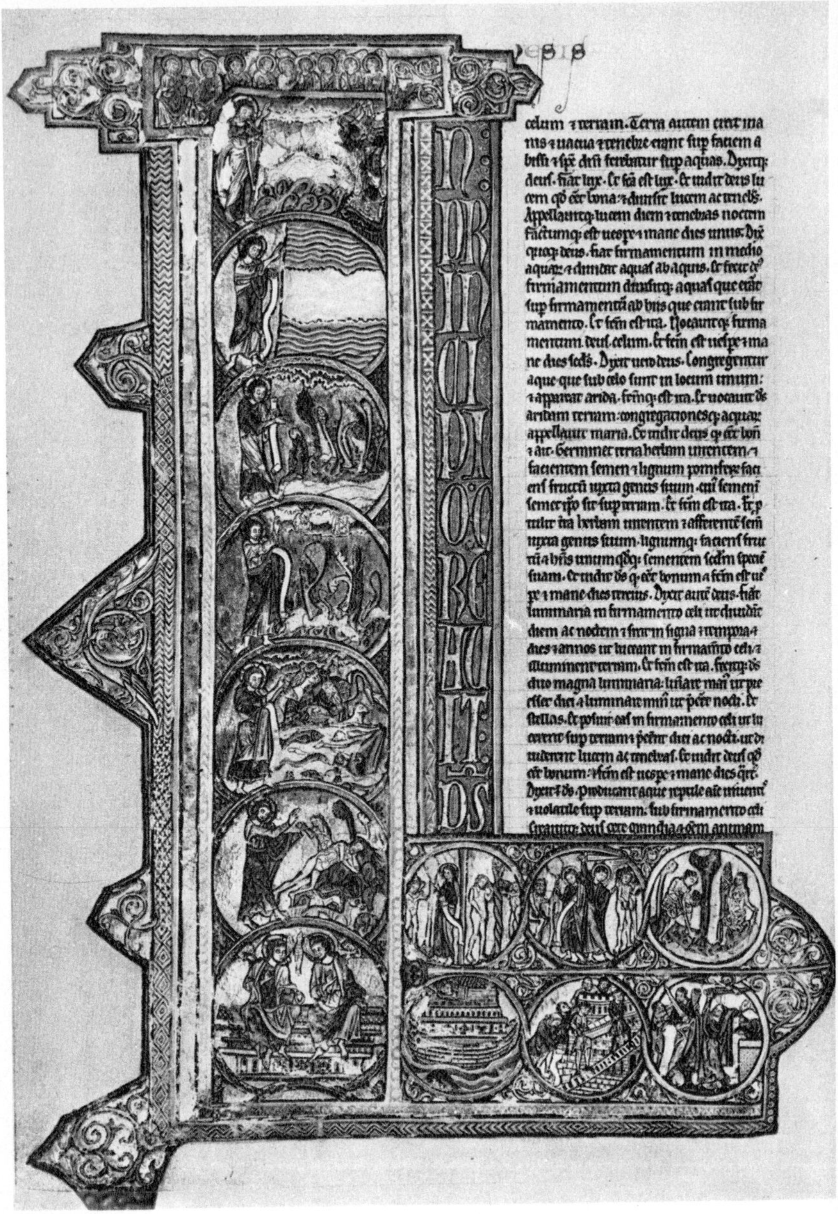

celum 7 terram. Terra autem erat ina
nis 7 uacua 7 tenebre erant sup faciem a
bissi 7 sps dei ferebatur sup aquas. Dyxitqz
deus. fiat lux. et fca est lux. et uidit deus lu
cem qd eet bona: 7 diuisit lucem ac tenebs.
Appellauitqz lucem diem 7 tenebras noctem
factumqz est uespe 7 mane dies unus. Dy
xit qz deus. fiat firmamentum in medio
aquaru: 7 diuidat aquas ab aquis. et fecit de̅
firmamentum diuisitqz aquas que erant
sup firmamentum ab his que erant sub fir
mamento. et fcm est ita. Uocauitqz firma
mentum deus celum. et fcm est uespe 7 ma
ne dies scds. Dyxit uero deus. Congregentur
aque que sub celo sunt in locum unum:
7 appareat arida. factumqz est ita. Et uocauit ds
aridam terram. congregationesqz aquaru
appellauit maria. Et uidit deus qd eet bon
7 ait. Germinet terra herbam uirentem
7 facientem semen 7 lignum pomiferu̅ fac
iens fructu̅ iuxta genus suum. cui semen
semetipso sit sup terram. et fcm est ita. Et p
tulit terra herbam uirentem 7 afferentem sem
iuxta genus suum. lignumqz faciens fru
ctum 7 h̅ns unumquodqz sementem sedm speciē
suam. Et uidit ds qd eet bonum. et fcm est u
spe 7 mane dies tercius. Dyxit aut̅ deus. fiat
luminaria in firmamento celi 7 diuidant
diem ac noctem 7 sint in signa 7 tempora
7 dies 7 annos ut luceant in firmamto celi 7
illuminent terram. et fcm est ita. fecitqz ds
duo magna luminaria: lu̅iare mai ut p̅
esset diei 7 luminare mi ut p̅esset nocti. et
stellas. et posuit eas in firmamento celi ut lu
cerent sup terram. 7 p̅essent diei ac nocti: 7 di
uiderent lucem ac tenebras. et uidit deus qd
eet bonum. et fcm est uespe 7 mane dies qrt̅.
Dyxit ds. producant aque reptile a̅e uiuentis
7 uolatile sup terram. sub firmamento celi
creauitqz deus cete grandia 7 om̅em anim̅a̅

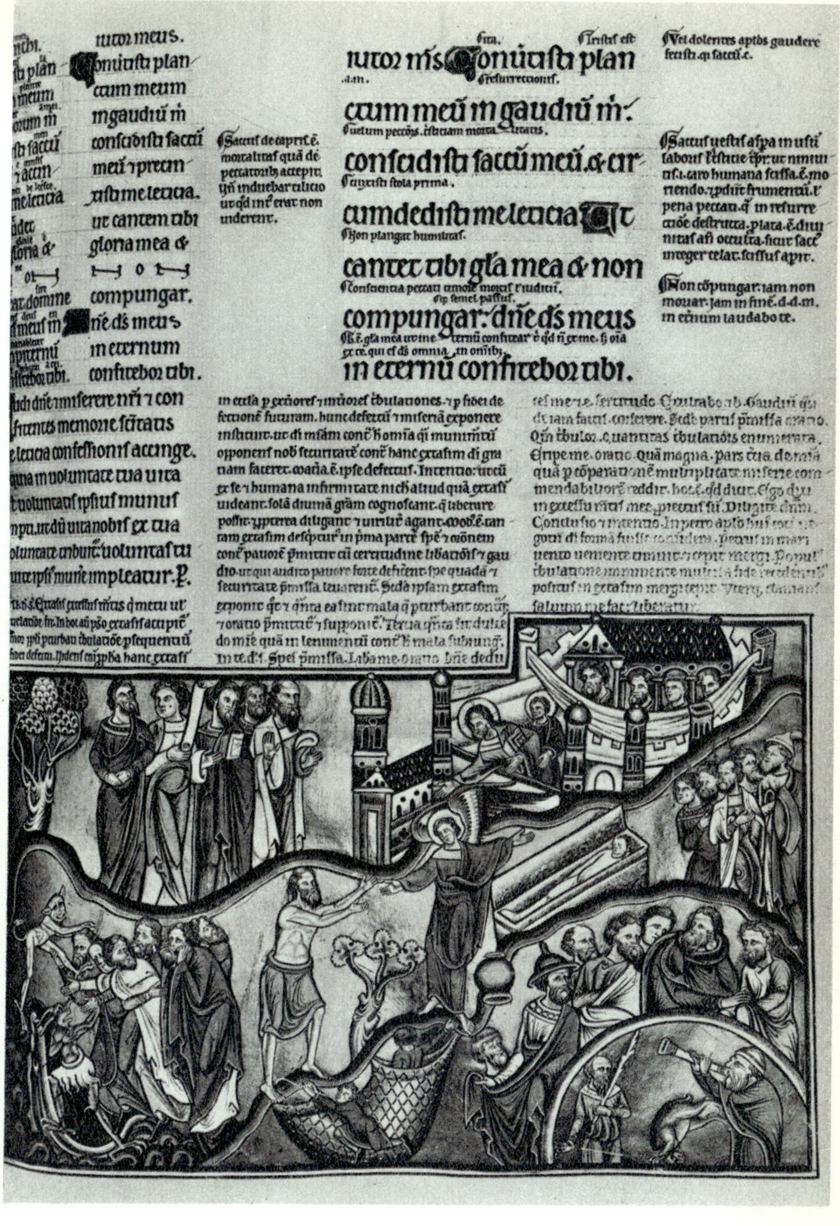
iutor meus.
Conuitisti plan
ctum meum
in gaudiũ m̃
conscidisti saccũ
meũ ⁊ precin
xisti me leticia.
ut cantem tibi
gloria mea &
compungar.
in eternum
confitebor tibi.
ctum meũ in gaudiũ m̃:
conscidisti saccũ meũ. & cir
cumdedisti me leticia: Ut
cantet tibi glã mea & non
compungar: dñe ds meus
in eternũ confitebor tibi.

Beatus uir qui non abiit
in consilio impiorum et
in uia peccatorum non
stetit: et in cathedra pesti
lencie non sedit.
Sed in lege domini uolū
tas eius: et in lege eius meditabi die ac nocte.
Et erit tanquam lignum quod plantatū e

MARCVS
LVCAS

O felicia oscula Lactentis labiis impressa. cū
FRĒ MATHIAS PARISIENSIS

103

d' helm ist uch benennet nicht.
noch and' wapfen noch d' schilt.
ob uch des vrowe nicht bevilt.
gebet mir sus unverstrite.
do gelobete im diu gehiwre.
von silb' von golde. von andrem solde.
des antwort ich dir genůch.
mer dan ich des ie gewůch.
Wolt ir nu horen wiez geste
umbe den zorn den ir hortet e.
über den zů rome brachte.
wie dem markise nachte
vrowede vn̄ hoher můt.
vn̄ wie ir lip vn̄ ir gůt.
vn̄ ir gunst mit herten sinne.
diu romische kuniginne.
mit truwen gap in sin gebot.
des was kyburge not.
ob dem markise wol gelanc.
den minne vn̄ iamer twanc.
waz pfandes her hi gelazen dort.
siu prubet ouch den guoten mort.
d' uf alyscanz gescach.
dar zů daz werltlich ungemach.
da kyburc inne bleip.
diu in nach helfe von ir treip.
kyburc was sin liebeste pfant.
nach ir im sin vrowde swant.
vn̄ gedultlichlich muse hi leben.
sin esse im nieman über geben.

105

Reges tharsis & insule munera offerēt.
ītrauerūt me aque usq; ad animā meā.

A obratiwssi se zase uzrela Gerisse · ale nepoznala · mniegici
by byl zahradnik · ptagicise naniem na Gerisse · A potom
poznawssi geho porzeczi · padla k geho noham · a Geris wecze · ne
dotikay se mne · Ale gdi k mim bratrzim · a powiez gim o mnie ·
A zatiem strazni ssedsse do miesta y prawili su to biskupom czo
se stalo · A oni poradiwsse se starssimi · dali mnoho penez gim ·
aby rzekli · ze ucedlnici prissedsse w nocy a my spime · ukradli
su geho · A ony wzewsse penieze · ucinili su tak · a to se wssudi rozhlasilo
Et conversa maria vidit Jhesum sed non cognovit putans
ortulanum · et postquam cognosceret eum per sermonem cecidit ad pedes eius Qui dixit
ei noli me tangere · sed vade ad fratres meos et dic eis veritatem ·

Ihc salutat matrem suā cum osculo pacis dicens
Salue mellita mea floscula vgo maria

sabbati aurea rutilatione resplenduit iuxta
quod psalmigraphus longe antea ꝓphetauit
Nox inquiens sicut dies illuminabitur Et
sic facta est hec nox illuminatio mea in delici
is meis . Iam subito michi dilectus filius asti
tit et refulgente inhabitaculo lumine his
uerbis me dulciter salutauit . Aue inquit
mater mi aue . Quasi dicat ve iam merens
depone quia sine ue me in utero concepisti et
sine doloris molestia uirgo ꝑmanens peperisti .
plangere desine lacrimas absterge gemitus re
pelle suspiria . Iam enim implete sunt scrip
ture quia oportuit me pati et a mortuis resur
gere . Iam prostrato ꝑncipe mortis infernum
exspoliaui potestatem in celo et terra accepi et
ouem perditam ad ouile pro humero repor
taui quia hominem qui perierat ad regna
celestia reuocaui . Gaude igitur mater aman
tissima quia facta es celi et terre regina .
Et sicut morte interueniente obtinui dominiū
inferorum sic ascensionis gloria refulgente
regnū accipiam supernorum . Ascendam igitur
ad patrem meum ut preparem me diligen
tibus locum . Tu autem surge dilecta mea co
lumba mea speciosa mea electa michi ꝑ pre
electa . Incipe iam in presenti gaudiū tibi in fu
turo longe gloriosius eternaliter ꝑmansurum . Isti
mo in montem syon matre cū discipulis con

Gen. 19.
Gen. 19.

properauerunt. quod nec retro ꝓspice-
rent. Ex hec autem euentu loc(us)
ille unde teutonici tam turpiter
de decorati. abiectis clipeis fuge-
runt. usq(ue) hodie wertesheghe nu(n)
cupatur. De coronacione Salomo
nis patre suo andrea rege adhuc
viuente.
Postquam autem cesar henricus
cum tanto dedecore fugit infra
suam de vngaria rex andreas mit
tens ad eum legatos petiuit ab
eo. ut sophiam filiam suã salo

N on putat. inuictos seuū destringē ferrum
Q uīq3 suos ciues qd signa adūsa tulerunt
N on credit fecisse nefas. Pompeius in arto
a gmina uix loco uetita ūtute moueri

Butirum.

117

Hymnus sanctorum & festorum. Ambrosij et Augustini. de sce trinitate.

Te deum laudamus. Te dominum confitemur. Te eternum patrem omnis terra ueneratur. Tibi omnes angeli et archangeli. tibi celi et uniuerse potestates. Tibi kerubim et seraphin incessabili uoce proclamant dicentes. Sanctus. Sanctus. Sanctus dominus deus sabaoth. Pleni sunt celi et terra maiestatis tue glorie. Te gloriosus apostolorum chorus. Te prophetarum laudabilis numerus. Te martyrum candidatus laudat exercitus. Te per orbem terrarum sancta confitetur ecclesia. Patrem inmense maiestatis. Venerandum tuum uerum et unicum filium. Sanctum quoque paraclitum spiritum. Tu rex glorie xpe. Tu patris sempiterni es filius. Tu ad liberandum suscepturus hominem non horruisti uirginis uterum. Tu de-

uicto mortis aculeo aperuisti credentibus regna celorum. Tu ad dexteram dei sedes in gloria patris. Iudex crederis esse uenturus. Te ergo quesumus tuis famulis subueni. quos precioso sanguine redemisti. Eterna fac cum sanctis tuis in gloria numerari. Saluum fac populum tuum domine. Et benedic hereditati tue. Et rege eos et extolle illos usque in eternum. Per singulos dies benedicimus te. Et laudamus nomen tuum in eternum et in seculum seculi. Dignare domine die isto sine peccato nos custodire. Miserere nostri domine miserere nostri. Fiat domine misericordia tua super nos quemadmodum sperauimus in te. Ipse domine speraui non confundar in eternum. Benedictus es domine deus patrum nostrorum. et laudabilis et gloriosus in secula seculorum. Amen.

Incipit liber psalterij secundum translationem scissimam ac uenerabilis patris nostri Ambrosij. sancte Mediolanensis ecclesie archiepiscopi. ps. dauid.

Beatus uir qui non habijt in consilio impiorum. et in uia peccatorum non ste-

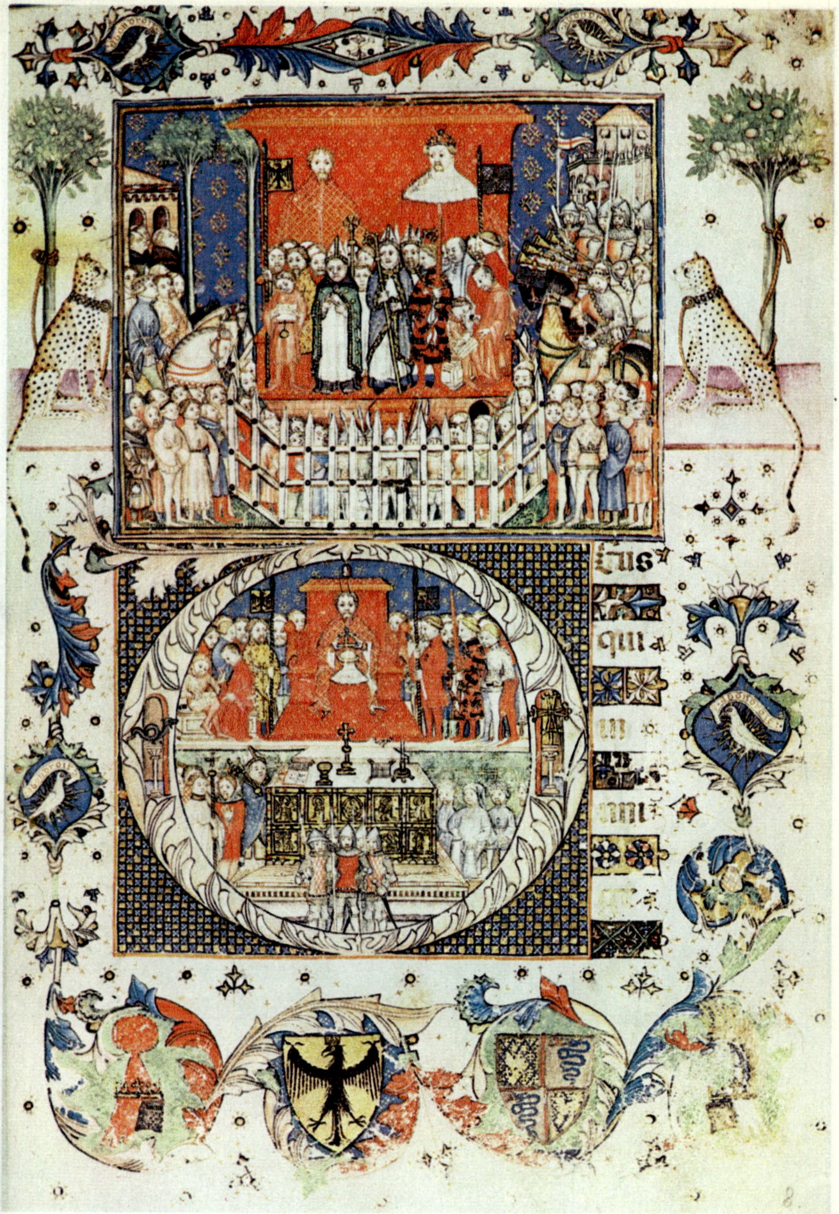

119

ad sepolcri de heretici ad aptar uocabulo che possa ipor
tar chiesa sacrata. Seguita nel testo.

tutti coperchi e nessun guardia face
Et quelli adme tutti saran serrati
quando di Josaffa qui torneranno
coicorpi chelassu anno lasciati
Suo cimitero daquesta parte anno
con Epicuro tutti suoi seguaci
chelanima colcorpo morta fanno
Pero aladimanda chemmi faci
quincentro satisfacto sara tosto
e aldisio ancor chetu mitaci

mio figlio ove e perche noe ci teco
Et io allui dame stesso nonuegno
cholui chattende la perqui mimena
forse chui guido uostro ebbe adisdegno
Le sue parole elmodo dellapena
mauean dicostui gia lecto ilnome
pero fu larisposta chosi piena
Di subito drizzato grido chome
dicesti egli ebbe nonuiue gli ancora
nonfiere gliocchi suoi lodolce lume

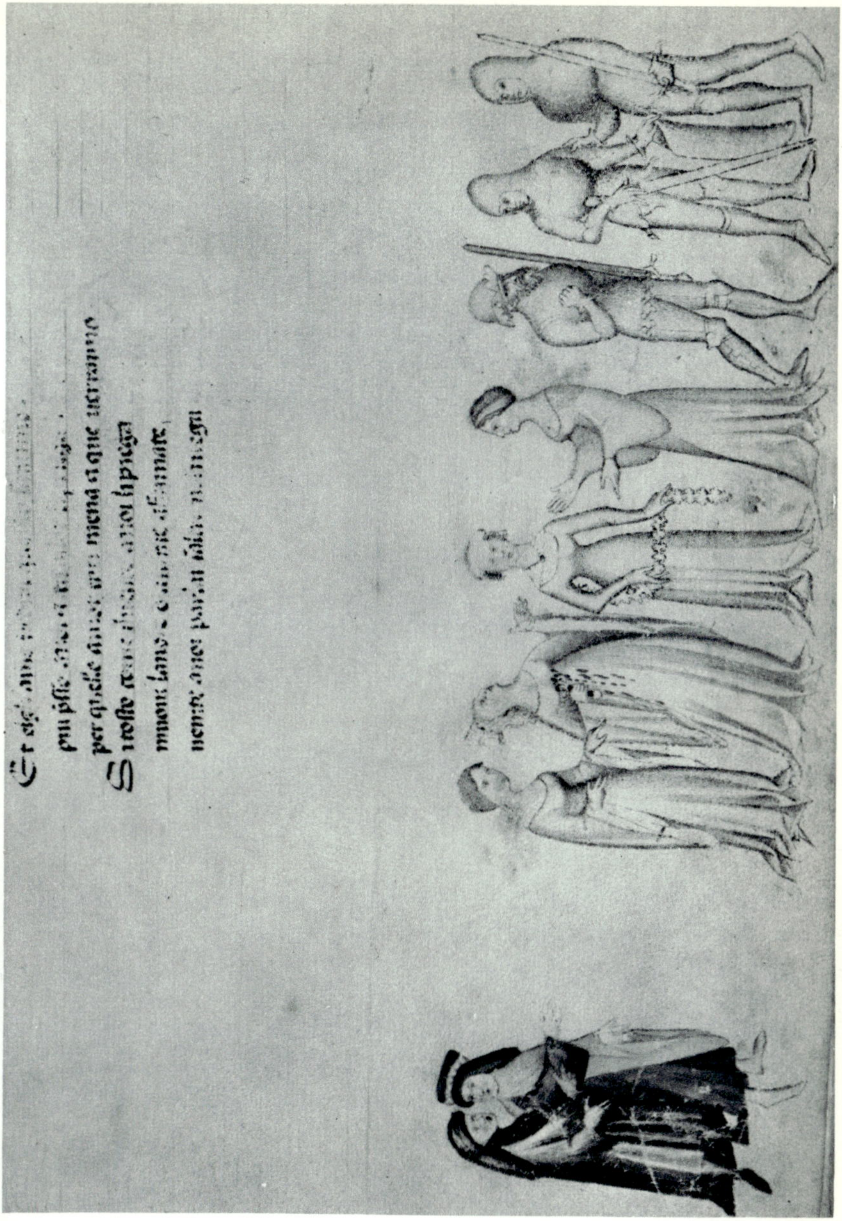

MARTINVS QVINTVS·ROMANVS PP BENIGNVS·HOC OPVS INSIGNE·PRESTANTI MVNERE DONAT·CVLPARVM VENIAM·FAMAM LONGEQ PER VRBES·CONTVLIT ETERNAM·PRESENTIA PRESVLIS ALMI·
A D M CCCC X X
est locus
iste hic domus de
e et porta celi et uo

127

e uentre matris mee uocauit me dñs
nomine meo. et posuit os meū sicut
gladium acutum sub tegumento
manus sue protexit me posuit me

Oratio de sancta maria.
Obsecro te domina sancta ma
ria mater dei pietate ple
nissima summi regis filia

131

Ad uesperas.
Deus in adiu
torium me
um intende
Domine ad adiuuā
dum me festina
Gloria patri et filio
et spiritui sancto

aproche aproche

Chy comenche le livre de mōs saīt
augustin de la cite de dieu Et p̄mier
Prologue epistolaire de lexpositeur
Vous tresex
cellant prince
Charles le quīt
Roy de france
Je raoul de
praelles vost
humble serviteur et subgiet
Tout vostre Et tout che que ie scay
et puys faire à vostre cōmandement
Mon tresredoubte seigneur Les
naturiens cōme pline Adelin Aristote Bede Et autres qui firent les
livres des proprietes des choses recitent laigle Roy souverain sus tous
les oisiaux Et entre ses proprietes
dient ilz a pluseurs li en attribuent
La premiere quelle surmōte en aage sur tous aultres oysiaux
La seconde quelle regarde directement
et sans flechir le soleil
La tierce que ses faons elle espreuve et ceulx qui ne
peuent regarder le soleil plainement
sans flechir elle les gette hors de son
ny et renye
Et quant iay bien
considere et ymagine ces trois haultes
proprietes Il me samble que je ne les
puys mieulx comparagier ne plus
proprement a nul de tous les docteurs
de sainte eglise especialment de leglise
primitive q̄ à mons saint augustin
Car premierement en la doctrine de la
foy en la confutacion ou reprobacion
des herites en la declaration de la benoite trinite oncques nulz de tous peulx

puincia huc aduenisti: vel quo
nomine vocaris. Sanctus ge
orgius dixit. xpianus & dei
seruus sum: georgius nuncu
por genere capadocius prie mee
comitatum gessi. Elegi vero
temporali carere dignitate: et
inmortalis dei impio deseruire.
Dacianus dixit. Erras
georgi: accede & im
mola deo appollini.
Beatus georgius respondit. Do
mino ihesu xpisto celi cultu
ram omnium seculorum: non appol

Eus in adiutoriũ
meũ intende
mine ad adiuuan

vii·xviii·
Le roy charles le
quint et la royne
Jehanne de bourbon
sa femme furent sacrez
en leglise de rains par messire
Jehan de craon archevesque le jour
de la trinite Lan lxiiii. Au quel
sacre furent le roy de chipre et
plusieurs ducs contes et barons puis
vindrent a paris a grant honneur
et noblesse et y eut Jouxtes et festes
moult honnorables. Le roy donna
lors la duche de bourgongne a
phelippe son frere qui lui en fist
hommage. Entre ces choses
bertran du glaiaquin chevalier

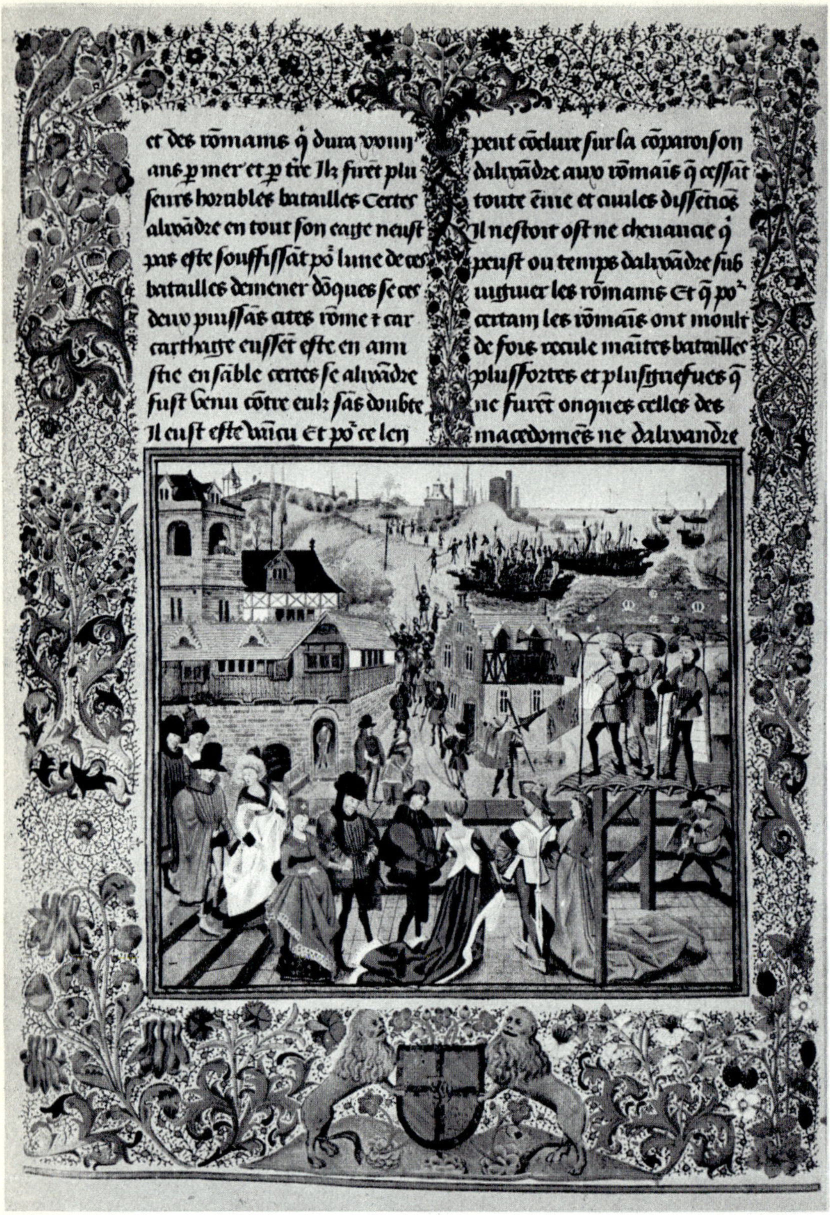
et des rōmains q̄ dura xviij
ans p mer et p tre Ilz furet plu
seurs horribles batailles Certes
alixādre en tout son eage neust
pas este souffissāt pō lune de ces
batailles demener donques se ces
deux puissās cites rome & car
carthage eussēt este en ami
stie ensāble certes se alixādre
fust venu cōtre eulz sās doubte
Il eust este vaincu Et pō ce len
peut cōclure sur la cōparoison
dalixādre aux rōmais q̄ cessat
toute ēvie et cavilles dissētiōs
Il nestoit ost ne chevanaie q̄
peust ou temps dalixādre sub
iuguier les rōmains Et q̄ pō
certain les rōmais ont moult
de fois recule maītes batailles
plus fortes et plus furieuses q̄
ne furēt onques celles des
macedoniēs ne dalixandre

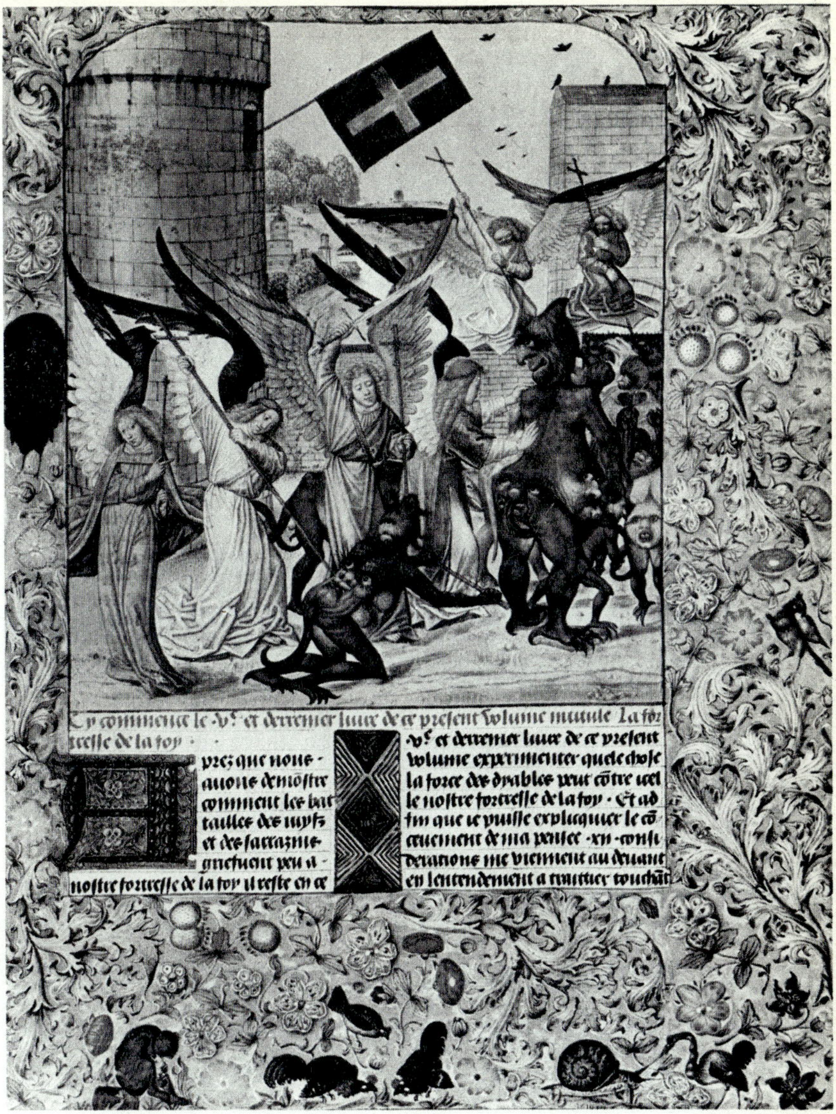

Cy commence le vi.° et derrenier liure de ce present volume intitulé La forteresse de la foy .

puis que nous
auions demostr
comment les bat
tailles des juifz
et des sarrazins
gnoient veu si
nostre forteresse de la foy il reste en ce

vi.° et derrenier liure de ce present
volume experimenter quelcquechose
la force des diables peut contre icel
le nostre forteresse de la foy . Et ad
fin que ie puisse expliquer le co
mencement de ma pensee xii consi
derations me viennent au deuant
en lentendement a traictier touchât

Hie wellen sich Jason vnd medea slafen legen · xxvii·

an geuat wan sölichs allein gotes ist in des hende sein gesetzt zu
wissen die zeit d' zeite vnd die augeplick · Was ist nu furbaß
do medea võ Jasone
aufnam den aid do
giengē si paide i das
slafgemach ein vn
gelaubigē wunsa
keit gezieret in abge
zognē klaidern pai
de nackendt · die nū
kkrawlichē gesloss
hat geoffent Jason
in der medea ·
Also ist durch si ver
zert die gantze un
ch i wunsame kurz
weilen der wollust
wie medea het er
fullet mit gening
thūē mer begir doch

das menlich vmfahe od' halsen vnd der begerēde vnkeusche tate
von Jasone · dennoch ist nit v
swunden der funck der begirlich
keit in jr · sunder durch die ver
suechtē tate nach dem hat er
fangē grossere entzundūgen
wen si vor der sundē hett · Das
ist der smag insemlich wun
samkeit versuret werde die du
rstigē liebhaber · welch gesm
ag so er ye mer gewonne wt
te mer er begirlich ist dē d' ge
sangte mage nit gehassen
mag · wañ die begirlichkeit
vñ geitikeit des wollustes

Hie legen Jason vnd medea by enander · xxviii·

hie werden Jason vnd hercules von dem kunig oeti entfangen
xiiii ·

Dat Jason vnd hercules mit iren geselle kuniglich zuchtlich vnd
eingezoge in eine gleiche wege habe sich zugefuret · welch im den
di gassen der stat in ein zwifache lenge irschinet messige schrit ei
ner loblichen schickung werde erkent · Es verwundt das volk sie su
zu leuchtet so vil kuniglich gepar · ein solich schon bluen der iuget
So sittlich in ire schriten · vnd in irem apparat i so vil site vbgen
ne · mit dirsteten gemute fragt das volk wer sind sie vo wanne sind
si · vnd was ist die sache irer zukunft · Al also fraget ist niemant

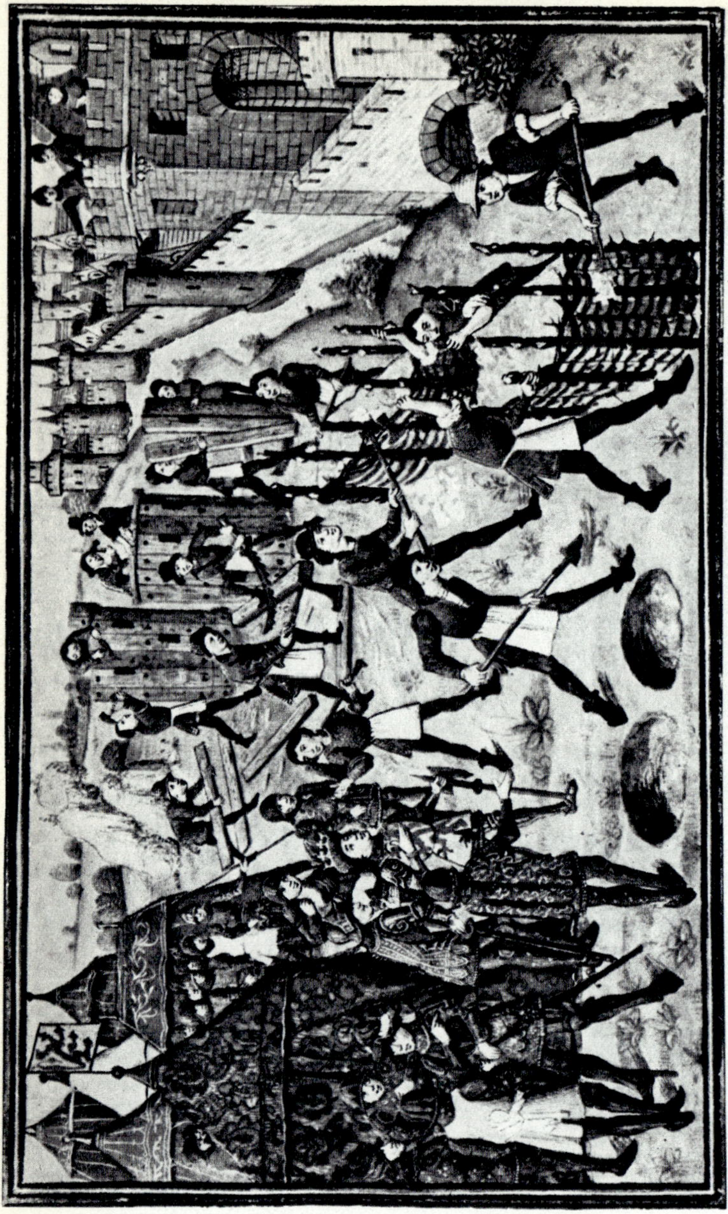

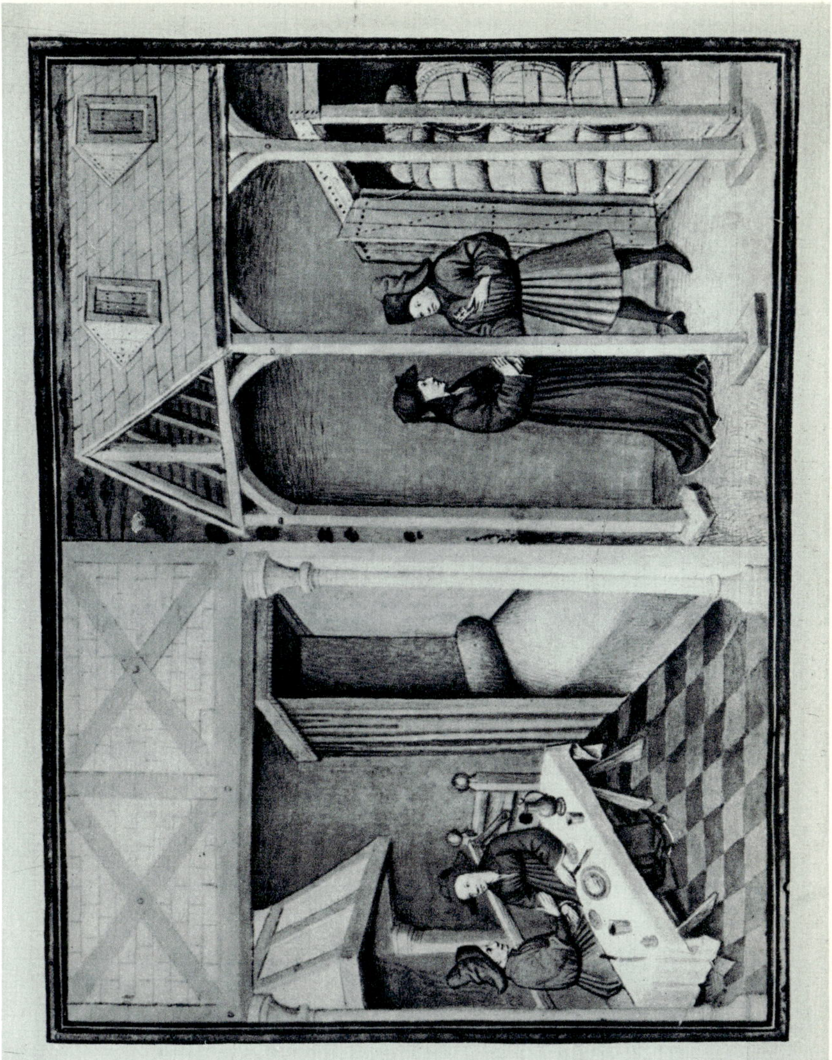

Pour che que par le record z ramembrãce de nobles emprises et fais darmes conquestes z vaillandises faites z achieuees par les vaillãs nobles z puissans hommes du tamps anchien z par chi deuant passet. les cuers des nobles z vaillans hommes du tamps pñt desirans et voellans attaindre la haulte z excellente vertu de proesche z de bonne renommee. sont esmeu es leue z mete plus en parfont a

Prologue de lacteur.
Les fais des anciens dont
on voulentiers lyre ouyr
et diligentement retenir
Car ilz peuent valoir et
donner bon exemple aux hardis en armes

ant. Placebo. ps.
ilexi quoniam
exaudiet do
minus: vocem

151

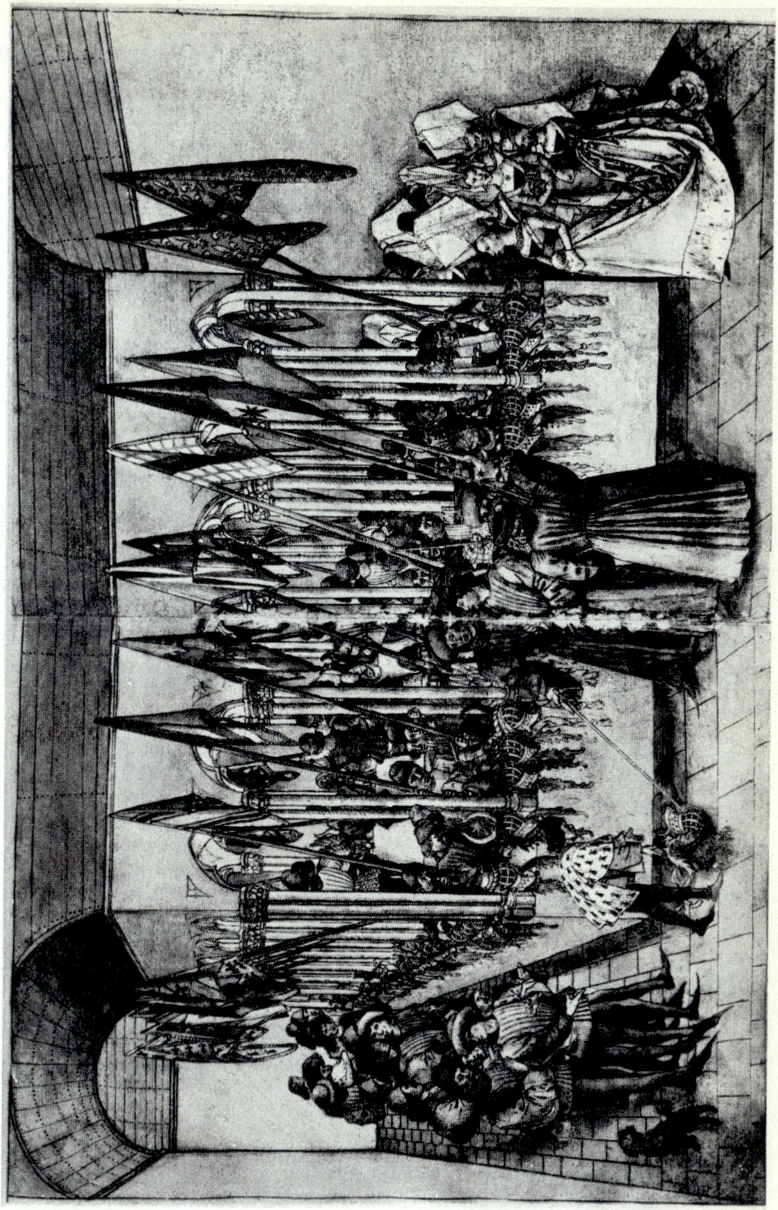

Droit et deuant soubz ce perron
De marbre noir comme charbon
Sourt la fontaine de fortune
Ou il n'ya quelle nesune
Et la fist compasser et faire
Vng tirant Joyant de faulx affaire

E soleil ja par deux foiz es
thrans montaignes auoit
fait fondre les neges Et au
tant de foiz zephirus auoit re
du les belles fleurs et fueilles

157

MAISTRE
ESTI ENNE
CHEVALIER
TEMPLUM

163

Apres que moyse se feust
ainsi parti des hommes
et le pleur en fu failli
et que les hebrieux eu
rent mise toute lesperance quilz a
uoient a luy en iosue. Josue com
manda que le peuple feust appareil
lie a bataillier et enuoya espieurs
en iherico pour scauoir leur uoule
te et leur uertu ad ce que ilz en eus
sent congnoissance. et il disposoit so
ost aussi comme sil voulsist trespas

Quant Richart filz
du duc Guillaume
longuespee lequel
estoit encore enfant
sceut la mort de son pere Si fu
moult dolant et fort a apaiser
selon laage quil avoit. Et
lors deux barons qui avoient
servi le duc Guillaume. lun
nommé Benart le danoiz
Quens de Rouen et lautre
Osmont Assemblerent les ba
rons de Normandie et de Bre
taigne et leur monstrerent
la maniere de la mort du duc
Guillaume et comme Richart
estoit son filz naturel et esto
leur droit seigneur Et comme
des le vivant du duc Guille
lui avoient fait hommaige
comme a leur droit seigneur
Surquoy les barons respondi
rent que voirement le tenoient
ilz a seigneur Et comme a le
seigneur obaissoient et le servi
roient et ordonnerent Benart
le danois a le gouverner. Ice
lui Benart estoit moult preu
domme et avoit moult justi
ce et estoit moult preux et har
di et sage chevalier. Il eust
a gouverner Normandie et
par telle maniere gouverna
que nul nosoit meffaire a lau
tre ne tollir riens. Et moult
fu grant nouvelle du bon gou
vernement et de la bonne justice
que len y faisoit. Et tres gra
cieusement se contenoit le
duc Richart et merveilleuse
ment ses gens le prindrent
a amer. Lan de lyncarna
cion nre seigneur ix c xlii as
commenca le duc Richart a

Photo B.N.

O martine o pie q
pium est gaudere
re de te. o martine

oys par la grace de dieu roy de france. Savoir
faisons a tous pns et advenir. Que pour
la tres parfaicte et singuliere amour que

INRI

INRI

INICIV SÂCTI EWANGELII SECVDVM LVCE